Performance and Ethnography

Performance and Ethnography: Dance, Drama, Music

Edited by

Peter Harrop and Dunja Njaradi

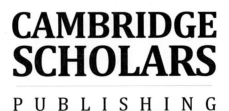
CAMBRIDGE SCHOLARS

P U B L I S H I N G

Performance and Ethnography: Dance, Drama, Music,
Edited by Peter Harrop and Dunja Njaradi

This book first published 2013

Cambridge Scholars Publishing

12 Back Chapman Street, Newcastle upon Tyne, NE6 2XX, UK

British Library Cataloguing in Publication Data
A catalogue record for this book is available from the British Library

ISBN (10): 1-4438-4761-5, ISBN (13): 978-1-4438-4761-2

TABLE OF CONTENTS

CHAPTER ONE

INTRODUCTION BY WAY
OF LONG ETHNOGRAPHY

PETER HARROP

Introduction

The chapters of this book were first presented as papers in July 2012 at *Traditional Performance— Contemporary Ethnography* at the University of Chester.[1] Most of our conference speakers had a background in performing arts, in dance, drama or music as well as performance studies. Several contributors also have varied and sometimes extended engagements—from different times and different places—with folklore, anthropology and ethnology. As Shannon Jackson points out in Professing Performance "scholars continually find themselves rehearsing and revising various kinds of intellectual histories [and] depending upon a prior disciplinary affiliation, some may emphasize certain figures over others."[2] Those affiliations, rehearsals, revisions and emphases, viewed through the lenses of ethnographic case study, are a feature of this collection which gathers together ideas, models and reflections within the broader discipline of performance studies. Originating from the performance orientation in folklore studies as well as Richard Schechner's now canonical collaboration with Victor Turner, performance studies "practice" brings together theatre and anthropology, privileging ethnography over spectatorship and process over product. The idea of "embodied ethnography" is never far away in

---

[1] The conference was convened by Peter Harrop and Dunja Njaradi with the support of the Performing Arts Department and Faculty of Arts and Media. A particular thanks to Professor Darren Sproston, Head of Performing Arts and Robin Gallie of the University Conference Office. The editors are particularly grateful to Shelley Hanvey for her assistance and familiarity with *how to geek*.

[2] Shannon Jackson, Professing Performance: Theatre in the Academy from Philology to Performativity (Cambridge: Cambridge University Press, 2004), 12.

these chapters, often evidencing new orientations and areas of performance research, but for the most part this volume aligns more closely to the ethnography of performance than to performance ethnography as presently conceived. The summer 2012 edition of *Canadian Theatre Review* comprised a special issue on Performance Ethnography which, while adopting more or less the same starting point as our conference, provides a complementary reflection on the possibility of performing the ethnography itself.[3] In a 2004 review essay Paul Atkinson remarked of Norman Denzin's *Performance Ethnography: Critical pedagogy and the Politics of Culture* that "There is a terrible danger, it seems to me, of collapsing the social world into one's own lifeworld."[4] The kinds of ethnographic engagement described in this volume indicate our contributors will have considered that central difficulty in one way or another, acknowledging a tension of essences between the social world and "lifeworld," but there is no unified or polemical sense of position on the matter.

By way of introduction I consider the emergence of the performance orientation in the folkloristics of the 1970's through to current trends in embodied ethnography via a durational approach to English traditions— the Long Ethnography of my title. Njaradi, originally trained as an anthropologist in Eastern Europe, revisits the Schechner/Turner collaboration to suggest new points of contact between performance and anthropology with particular reference to ritual and magic. David explores how the emplaced body can yield deeper levels of understanding and insight through engaged practice on different levels, using several detailed examples from her fieldwork with Hindu dancers in the UK as well as her current fieldwork in Bhutan. Bacon suggests a partly complementary yet partly antagonistic position whereby Performance Studies forms a theoretical space for self and other, for analysis and practice, predicated on her

---

[3] *Canadian Theatre Review* 151, 2012, Performance Ethnography. See particularly Brian Rusted, "Introduction: From Ethnography of Performance to Performance Ethnography," 3-6 and Virginie Magnat, "Can Research Become Ceremony? Performance Ethnography and Indigenous Epistemologies," 30 – 36. The TPQ symposium on Performance Ethnography in Text and Performance Quarterly 44, no. 4 (2006) also contains helpful material, particularly John T. Warren, "Introduction: Performance Ethnography," 317-319 and Della Pollock, "Marking New Directions in Performance Ethnography," 325-329.

[4] Paul Atkinson, "Review Essay, Performing ethnography and the ethnography of performance," British Journal of Sociology of Education 25, no. 1 (2004): 107-114. Atkinson reviews Norman K. Denzin, Performance Ethnography: Critical Pedagogy and the Politics of Culture (Thousand Oaks; London; New Delhi: Sage Publications, 2003).

research with English Arabic dancers and with spirituality, moving to ask the question "what if I ask those questions of myself?" The final three chapters are more clearly defined case studies. Quigley commences a preliminary anthropology of Performance Studies itself via the ethnography of three Performance Studies international conferences. Power takes a different angle on embodied, situated knowledge, looking at the Scottish smallpipe revival to explore the artisanal production of musical instruments as performance. Power argues that the ideology of an artisanal musical maker is congealed in his instruments and carried forward to the drastic moment of musical performance. Smith takes a historical perspective to examine the commodification of mumming traditions in Newfoundland, Canada, from performative frameworks for sustained systems of localised work relations, into domestic tourist attraction.

Books and Fieldwork

What follows is the communication of a scrapbook, the weaving together of memories and separately acquired ideas, four postcards sent at different times from different places, but all addressing the same three things. Firstly; my response to traditional folkloric performance—the mummer's play; secondly, the various ideas and bodies of knowledge that the performers and their audiences hold about that tradition; thirdly, the scholarship that seeks to contextualise, record and make sense of that.[5] The potential for or even appropriateness of the integration of performance, performers, spectators and ethnographer-scholars (and the last three are by no means mutually exclusive) is probably the central issue of this volume. In the original conference call we asked whether it was possible to achieve an embodied, affective and sensory ethnography and whether we are shaped by engagement with ethnographic practice, by the relationship between self, duration, tradition and change. I called my symposium paper Long Ethnography since it charted a forty year engagement with mumming. Although I've eventually focussed on one village in the north west of England, and a local variant of mumming known as Soulcaking, my broader and current concern is actually the intersection of site, memory and performance as revealed by ethnography.[6]

---

[5] For those unfamiliar with the activity of mumming the following websites provide an introduction and overview as well as considerable local and specific detail: http://www.mastermummers.org/ and http://www.folkplay.info/
[6] Peter Harrop, "The Antrobus Soulcakers: A consideration of site, mobility and time as components of traditional performance," Contemporary Theatre Review 22, no. 2 (2012): 267-273.

In re-presenting that work as an introductory chapter for this volume I also
consider the extent to which the Victorian idea of survival in culture, the
more recent performance orientation in folkloristics and lastly critical
theory, continue to haunt the contemporary. The performance orientation
certainly had a profound influence on academic folklore during a "long
1960's," as well as forming part of the nexus of thought that became
Performance Studies. The movement encouraged reflection on fieldwork
and method while theorising the importance of the context and
performance of folklore, the act of folklore, in determining what folklore
might mean. *Survival in culture* on the other hand, is shorthand for an
earlier and persistent frame of reference posited by Edward Tylor in
Primitive Culture in 1871, and exemplified and popularised by James
Frazer in his later work *The Golden Bough*.[7] The basis of Tylor's
argument can be summarised thus: traditional customs and folklore were
the survivals of ancient beliefs, rituals and ceremonies which had, until
more recently, survived in less fragmented form in those cultures least
influenced by European thought. (Hence: The *Ur-form* is always either
temporally or culturally distant from *us* as an opaque expression of social
Darwinism.) Lastly it has become increasingly difficult to consider
folklore *per se* without some acknowledgement of repetition and
différance.[8] A reflective consideration of these various scholarly shifts that
have overlapped and influenced my own approaches—hopefully in the
spirit of auto-ethnography rather than egocentricity—may be of value in
positioning the very different contributions that make up this volume.

It is now commonplace to remark that the idea of survival in culture
has itself become a survival in culture every bit as atavistic as the ritual
survivals described by Tylor et al. What is less frequently considered is the
extent to which those ideas have entered the fabric of contemporary
traditional custom. Contemporary folklorists have accepted the extent to
which the interpretation of custom offered by Frazer is used to explain
traditional custom by the occasionally interested lay observer, but what

---

[7] Edward B. Tyler, Primitive Culture, Researches into the Development of
Mythology, Philosophy, Religion, Art and Custom, 2 vols. (London: J. Murray,
1871); James G. Frazer, The Golden Bough, A Study in Comparative Religion, 2
vols. (London: Macmillan, 1894).
[8] Différance is a French term coined by Jacques Derrida, deliberately homophonous
with the word "difference." Différance plays on the fact that the French word
différer means both "to defer" and "to differ." It is particularly apposite in folklore
where there has been an emphasis on matters of textual and performative diffusion
and variation.

often exasperates the same folklorists is the popularity of that rationale among the exponents of the traditions under study, and this is especially vexing when those people are *very like* the folklorists. (Cheshire, for example, is short on savages and savage customs, lacking in peasants and peasant belief—to paraphrase the title of Richard Dorson's classic history of the British Folklorists—so a certain kind of folklorist or local historian might be forgiven for thinking *these people should know better!*)[9] The idea of "ancientness" has so permeated traditional performance in England that an absence of evidence can become much more compelling for the participants (actors and audiences) than the folklorists' "prize-find" letter confirming that a particular activity was first undertaken in 1908 rather than during the bronze-age. What we have here is a blurring of the item of folklore within the performance of a "metafolklore" whereby the original item of folklore is performed as though a subsequent explanation were the grounds for its existence in the first place. Folklorists are themselves traditionally accepting of people's reasons for doing things even when confident that the thing "those people" are doing isn't what "those people" think it is, and that their reason for doing it is therefore suspect. Allow me the following fictitious conversation: "This morris dance has gone on here for hundreds of years" states the morris dancer. "No it hasn't," responds the folklorist, "it first took place in May 1908, after the son of the big house went to Cambridge, read Frazer, and discovered that morris dancing was the remnant of an ancient fertility rite, and thought the village should have some. Look, he outlines his plans in this letter to his sister dated November 1907." "What do you academics know about it?" responds the morris dancer, herself a graduate, "This morris dance has gone on here for hundreds of years. Haven't you read Frazer or seen the Wicker Man?" Perhaps there is a performance theology out there, somewhere over the rational rainbow, desperately seeking a secular spirituality?

The Performance Orientation

In 1963 when the distinguished American folklorist Richard Dorson wrote a review of the then current trends in Folklore theory he was able to identify five dominant schools of thought: comparative, the national, the

---

[9] Richard M. Dorson, The British Folklorists: A History (London: Routledge and Kegan Paul, 1968) and Peasant Customs and Savage Myths: Selections from the British Folklorists, 2 vols. (Chicago and London: University of Chicago Press and Routledge Kegan Paul, 1968).

anthropological, the psychological, and the structural.[10] Nine years later, in 1972, he re-worked the essay and found it necessary to append a discussion of what he termed the contextual approach to folklore, which by the late 1970's was being comfortably referred to as the performance orientation in folklore.[11] What prompted him to re-think the work? The 37th International Congress of Americanists was held in Argentina in 1966 and led, for the folklorists, to the publication of two volumes of material which they noted as reaffirming broadly distinctive hemispheric approaches. The North American material, edited by Americo Paredes and Richard Bauman, appeared first in a special edition of the *Journal of American Folklore*[12] which the American Folklore Society quickly republished as *Toward New Perspectives in Folklore*.[13] As varied as the material was, the following passage from Baumann's introduction acknowledged and addressed a central theme:

> It may be useful to indicate the principal concerns that appear to us to emerge from the work as a whole. Of these, the most comprehensive is a full-scale and highly self-conscious reorientation from the traditional focus upon folklore as "item"—the things of folklore—to a conceptualisation of folklore as "event"—the doing of folklore. In particular there is an emphasis upon performance as an organising principle that comprehends within a single conceptual framework artistic act, expressive form, and aesthetic response, and that does so in terms of locally defined, culture specific categories and contexts.

Three years after the Buenos Aires conference, but still pre-dating the subsequent publications, the 1969 meeting of the Society, held in Atlanta, Georgia, continued to move that agenda along. Papers from Dell Hymes, Barbara Kirshenblatt-Gimblett and Bruce Rosenburg among others, later formed the nucleus of a published collection edited by Dan Ben-Amos and

---

[10] Richard M. Dorson, "Current Folklore Theories," Current Anthropology 4, (1963): 93-112. Dorson utilises these five sub-headings to structure his essay.
[11] Richard M. Dorson, ed., Folklore and Folklife: An Introduction (Chicago: University of Chicago Press, 1972), 45-47 and subsequent notes 12 to 14 below.
[12] Americo Paredes and Richard Bauman, eds., "Special Edition," Journal of American Folklore 84, (1971).
[13] Americo Paredes and Richard Bauman, eds., Toward New Perspective in Folklore (Austin: American Folklore Society, 1971). See particularly Americo Paredes, Foreword, iii – iv; and Richard Bauman, "Introduction," v – ix. (The Latin American work, co-edited by Americo Paredes and Manuel Dannemann was published in 1972 as El Estado Actual del Folklore en Latinamerica).

Kenneth Goldstein.[14] Although *Folklore: Performance and Communication* wasn't published until 1975 it eventually confirmed the contextual turn of *Toward New Perspectives in Folklore* and provided the impetus for Dorson's re-evaluation. Here are Ben-Amos and Goldstein from the co-authored introduction to the later work:

> The import of such a shift in focus from text to context for folklore studies...involves a conceptualisation of folklore in which communication and performance are key terms. It releases folklore from the literary bonds imposed upon it in archives and libraries and views it as human verbal symbolic interaction of a performing kind.[15]

In his contributory essay Breakthrough into Performance, Dell Hymes suggested that "one might even hope that folklore would take the lead in showing how appreciation and interpretation of performances as unique events can be united with analysis of the underlying rules and regulations which make performance possible and intelligible."[16] Folklore did take that lead in the USA where it is widely acknowledged as a major precursor for Performance Studies. In the UK the impact of the performance orientation was most strongly felt in the Institute for Dialect and Folk Life Studies (IDFLS) at the University of Leeds, and the Centre for English Cultural Tradition and Language (CECTAL) of the University of Sheffield. There were only ever a handful of Folklore "centres" in English universities (certainly not Departments) and the outcome of the 1979 general election led to a rapid series of University funding cuts which largely ended the development of Folklore in the English Academy. Furthermore, there has never been a consistent folkloric, anthropological or even social scientific presence in UK performing arts departments and that, coupled with a locally pervasive ahistoricism, sustains the performance orientation lacunae and represents a small academic "forgetting." This leaves us a UK Performance Studies focussed on, as Roms phrases it, "a privileging of the living avant garde and innovative, interdisciplinary aesthetic practices" rather than engaging with the North American broad spectrum approach.[17]

[14] Dan Ben-Amos, and Kenneth S. Goldstein, ed., Folklore: Performance and Communication, Issue 40 of Approaches to semiotics (The Hague: Mouton & Co., 1975).
[15] Ibid., 2-10.
[16] Dell Hymes, "Breakthrough into Performance," in Folklore: Performance and Communication, Issue 40 of Approaches to semiotics, ed. Dan Ben-Amos and Kenneth S. Goldstein (The Hague: Mouton & Co., 1975), 11.
[17] Heike Roms, "The Practice Turn: Performance and the British Academy," in Contesting Performance: Global Sites of Research, ed. Jon McKenzie, Heike

There is a lingering sense here in the UK (despite the clarity of, for example, Marvin Carlson's *Performance*)[18] that Schechner's *Between Theater and Anthropology* came from nowhere in the mid-eighties, as though that work had no context or antecedents outside of either eponymous discipline.[19]

Notwithstanding, between 1978 and 1986 two series' of conferences looking at Traditional Drama and Traditional Dance were held at the University of Sheffield and at Crewe and Alsager College of Higher Education respectively.[20] As far as I know these were the first manifestation of the performance orientation in the UK, and arguably the first Performance Studies in the UK, deriving from the two English Folk Life centres and explicitly concerned with English traditional performance forms. In focussing (largely) on mumming, morris and related performances, these conferences brought together academics and practitioners from drama, dance, folklore, history, geography, anthropology, linguistics and computing sciences. Some of the papers from the first of those events, *Traditional Drama 1978*, were published in 1985 with a preface by Paul Smith and John Widdowson of the Sheffield University CECTAL Traditional Drama Research Group. I'll quote at some length:

> Much discussion has concentrated on reconstructing the source of the actions of the plays in the religious rituals of prehistory. Over the past decade, however, criticism has been levelled at the employment of such abstract, unsubstantiated theory and also at the total neglect of any aspect of the performance of plays. This criticism has in turn fostered an expansion of research in traditional drama at all levels and pure dissatisfaction has led to the development of several alternative orientations in the scholarship. These range from [...] studies of performances in context [...] newer approaches to the subject [...] the theoretical premises

---

Roms, and C.J.W.-L. Wee, 51-70 (London: Palgrave Macmillan, 2010), 63. See also Peter Harrop, "What's in a Name? A Comparison of UK and US Performance Studies," Studies in Theatre and Performance 25, no. 3 (2005): 189-201.
[18] Marvin Carlson, Performance: A Critical Introduction (London: Routledge, 1996).
[19] Richard Schechner, Between Theater and Anthropology (Philadelphia: University of Pennsylvania Press, 1985).
[20] The Traditional Drama conferences at CECTAL, University of Sheffield, were convened by PhD student Paul Smith, presently Professor of Folklore at St Johns Memorial University, Newfoundland, Canada. The Traditional Dance conferences were convened by Theresa Buckland, then a PhD student at IDFLS and Lecturer at Crewe and Alsager, now Professor of Dance History and Ethnography, Roehampton University, UK.

which shape the study of the plays, examinations of contemporary performances and analytical techniques.[21]

The first Traditional Dance Conference was convened by Theresa Buckland, then concluding related doctoral research at the Leeds IDFLS, at Crewe and Alsager College in 1981. The edited proceedings were published the following year and the first paper was Buckland's *English Folk Dance Scholarship: A Review*.[22] These passages further illustrate the barely contained incredulity she shared with Smith and Widdowson:

> He [Needham] agreed with Phillips Barker that the processional forms were the earliest and gave them a Celtic origin and, dismissing indigenous pagan origins for the sword dance, he returned to the nineteenth century view that the sword dances were imported from Scandinavia. Although Needham gave England's dance forms ethnic identity, all were still interpreted as vestiges of pre-Christian religious festivals. None of his ethnic groups arrived here after 1066 yet all of Needham's examples date from 1800 at the earliest. He used mainly nineteenth century evidence to support what can be termed a pre-Norman Conquest invasions theory. [And] they [Thurston and the Fletts] sensibly demonstrated that a knowledge of post-mediaeval dance culture in order to understand folk dance is far more important than reflecting upon unknown pre-Christian ceremonies.[23]

These two series' of conferences cumulatively produced over eighty papers and achieved a good deal more than the critique of survivalism. In the development of Dance Studies one can see considerable strides have been taken through persistent work in the development of ethnochoreology (particularly the International Council for Traditional Music, Study Group on Ethnochoreology) and dance ethnography.[24] Work on British traditional drama has largely and stubbornly resisted the "theory explosion" although there has been growth in historical, regional and diasporic studies. The particular progress in enhancing understanding of traditional dance may

---

[21] Paul Smith and J.D.A. Widdowson, "Traditional Drama Studies", in Traditional Drama Studies Volume 1, Centre for English Cultural Tradition and Language and the Traditional Drama Research Group, ed. Paul Smith and J.D.A Widdowson (Doncaster: January Books, 1985), 3.

[22] Theresa Buckland, "English Folk Dance Scholarship: A Review," in Traditional Dance, vol. 1, ed. Theresa Buckland (Crewe and Alsager College, 1982).

[23] Ibid., 12-13.

[24] See International Council for Traditional Music, "Study Group on Ethnochoreology," http://www.ictmusic.org/group/ethnochoreology. The study group currently has 171 members, from over 45 nations.

have stemmed in part from Buckland's pan-European consciousness within the Study Group on Ethnochoreology. For myself, with a background in drama, it is relatively straightforward to see differences between a UK and a US Performance Studies, but I suggest that dance/performance studies, unlike drama/performance studies, has had a third engagement with broader European thought, cuing a further range of affiliations, rehearsals, revisions and emphases that have gone some way to realising Dell Hymes hopes. The following extract from our original call for papers tried to reflect this:

> Performance studies in America, thus, were developing by carefully examining the models of performance behaviours and processes useful not only to artists and theatre scholars but to anthropologists, folklorists, play theorists etc...Schechner's seminal study *Between Theater and Anthropology* underlines the ways in which performances could be seen as key paradigms for social processes—and popularised the now famous analogy between performance behaviour and ritual. Performance Studies in continental Europe (although we do acknowledge country-to-country differences) broadly followed American perspectives on performance albeit from different traditions. Deeply rooted in the nineteenth-century interest in the "national" and "folk," exemplified by a romanticised notion of the "peasant society," European ethnology/anthropology easily embraced the idea of cultural/social performance in which a culture plays out aspects of its world through symbolic performative displays such as folk dance and drama and related ritual behaviour. Although performance studies in continental Europe maintained the separation between studies of theatre/art performance and national/ritual/folk style performances the balance between these scholarships is, perhaps, better achieved than in the UK.[25]

Those earlier UK conferences have provided a notional base point for considering what the intervening thirty years of performance studies has brought to the table when it comes to appreciating and understanding the amateur, traditional, popular, particular, local, folkloric, fakeloric, competitive, unfashionable and nearly forgotten to scholarship. Before moving on to look at the response we received, however, a further note on (my) survival in culture.

---

[25] I am grateful to my colleague Dunja Njaradi, postdoctoral fellow in Performing Arts at the University of Chester, for the wording of this paragraph which formed part of a joint call for papers for the conference *Contemporary Ethnography— Traditional Performance,* University of Chester, July 13th/14th, 2012.

Ancient Mystery, Critical Theory and the Exotic

In 1968 I was persuaded by different friends to join a youth theatre and a folk dance club. Both of these organisations were products of their time and place, themselves subject to particular sets of conditions. On the one hand the youth theatre emphasised confidence and fluency in performative improvisation within a frame of ensemble work and the creation of atmosphere through a collective physicality and vocal presence. With hindsight the work reacted against the "talking heads" theatre of the day and embraced apparently "freer" yet more "ritualistic" action. Our teachers were part of the temper of the times in experimenting with the ideas of Brecht and Artaud. Of course I didn't think about it at the time; it was pleasingly experiential by comparison with school science, and differently experimental, and there were more girls there. In the morris men, on the other hand, we were drilled in the rapper sword dance and its percussive footwork. The revival and survival of this Tyneside sword dance was the raison d'être of the group, but we also undertook theatrical performance of dances and calendar customs from around England, often performing during interludes at social dancing events. The leader of the group owned copies of *The Sword Dances of Northern England* and *English Ritual Drama: A Geographical Index*, so the dancing already held a trace of ancient mystery for me, an imagined temporal exotic.[26] I was introduced to a variant of the Yorkshire Longsword dance (from the village of Ampleforth as recorded by Sharp)[27] which had a mummers' play attached. At midday on New Year's Day in 1971, in a new venture, we cleared the snow from a car park between two public houses, put salt down, got a crowd and danced. The "tradition" has sustained ever since.

When I was reading for my first degree the referencing of the mummers play in both scholarly and popular literature, whether anthropological, theatre historical or folkloric was almost entirely contextualised by the doctrine of survivals. I wasn't aware of the work of Herbert Halpert, Graham Story or Henry Glassie, but I was aware of the work of Alan Brody.[28] While I was trying to find ways to incorporate mumming into my

---

[26] Cecil J. Sharp, The Sword Dances of Northern England (East Ardsley : E.P. Publishing, 1977) and Christopher Cawte, Alex Helm and Norman Peacock, English Ritual Drama: A Geographical Index (London: The Folk-Lore Society, 1977).
[27] Sharp, 50-76.
[28] I've noted elsewhere that for a few years during the late 1960's and into the 1970's two parallel worlds seemed to exist in mumming scholarship. At the same

undergraduate projects, I was also being introduced to a more fashionable grapple with "the other." In 1931 Antonin Artaud had visited the Colonial Exposition in Paris where the Netherlands exhibit consisted of a Gamelan Orchestra and dancers from Bali, the Hindu enclave of the then Dutch East Indies, now Indonesia. In 1935 Bertolt Brecht visited Moscow and saw a performance by the Chinese actor Mei Lanfang. As a student of theatre in the 1970's these moments came to seem almost Damascene and carried a powerful suggestion that the authentic might be found in the traditional of the other. Grotowski's *via-negativa* and Barba's *pre-expressivity,* Brook's multi-cultural casting for *Orghast* and *The Ik* seemed impossibly exotic and distant, mysterious and romantic. Poland—still behind the iron curtain, Iran and Uganda. I had copies of works by Artaud, Frazer and Colin Turnbull (the anthropologist whose writing on The Ik people prompted Brook's work) on the go at the same time.[29] Writing in 1968 Dorson spoke of the period immediately following the Great War as being the point —in British Folklore—where "survivals gave way to revivals."[30] It seemed to me that the authentic, ancient and mysterious had slipped through our fingers, leaving a residue of Cecil Sharp and the English Folk Dance and Song Society. Where did that leave the authentic in the traditional of my culture? Did geographical and cultural distance make other "traditionals" more "traditional" than my own? Authenticity lingered in Brecht-and-Artaud land, in Paris-and-Moscow land, where interesting people became even more interesting by meeting Balinese and Chinese performers. There was little of that for me in 1970s Northumberland or Yorkshire—if the truth was out there it required airfare that I didn't have.

As an undergraduate I never realised that the demolition of survivalism was already under way, or grasped that the construction of a "canonical intercultural" was in full swing, and on one level it didn't matter. There was a feeling I got when I performed which I liked. It was to do with ensemble, and shared seriousness of purpose, and getting things right, and

---

time as Herbert Halpert and Graham Story were undertaking their pioneering study [Christmas Mumming in Newfoundland (Toronto: University of Toronto Press, 1969)] Alan Brody was still pursuing ancient mysteries with little sense of local context or meaning [The English Mummers and their Plays: Traces of Ancient Mystery (London: Routledge and Kegan Paul, 1969)]. Within six years Henry Glassie had confirmed the shift in emphasis [All Silver and no Brass: An Irish Christmas Mumming (Indiana: Indiana University Press, 1975)].

[29] For a full discussion of these trends and influences see Ric Knowles, Theatre and Interculturalism (Basingstoke: Palgrave Macmillan, 2010).

[30] Dorson, *The British Folklorists*, 448.

being good and showing off, and having fun, and having things to celebrate with other people. But certainly in my case there was also a particular attraction to the transitoriness and associated melancholy of calendar based performance. I learned experientially that the intersection of time and place could add powerful weight to performance and that was confirmed by my reading of performance history. The feeling grew stronger with repetition and my twin interests in drama and performance and folklore and performance gradually turned into one interest in performance anthropology reaffirmed through extended university study and a fieldwork based PhD on mumming. But of course this is not a narrative of integrations.

Towards the end of Francis Ford Coppola's 1979 film *Apocalypse Now*,[31] once we're in the real jungle, upriver and over-the-border no-man's land, we hear Kurtz reading the poetry of T S Eliot. The camera pans Kurtz's desk sufficiently slowly for the viewer to see two other works, both referenced in Eliot's notes to *The Waste Land*.[32] These are *The Golden Bough* by Sir James George Frazer, first published in two volumes in 1890 and almost certainly known to Conrad who serialised *The Heart of Darkness* (which story *Apocalypse Now* loosely retells) before publishing a full version in 1902.[33] Frazer developed the work and it was re-published in twelve volumes between 1906 and 1915, becoming an influential work which both fed and misrepresented the work of the "Great School" of British Folklorists in the popular imagination of the time. The final text on Kurtz's shelf is Jessie Weston's *From Ritual to Romance*, tracing the survival in culture of the idea of the Holy Grail.[34] As we've seen, those scholars were part of a movement holding the view that the interplay of myth and ritual in ancient and "primitive" cultures had given rise to modern religion and that echoes—somewhat like the big bang radiation reputedly present in the static on our analogue TV screens—were to be found in the folklore of the "advanced nations" and in the rites and rituals of "primitive peoples." Hence, we have the doctrine of "survivals" in culture and an "explanation" for almost every English folk custom. By the late 1970's this was finally being demolished by fieldwork, "grounded

[31] *Apocalypse Now*, IMDb www.imdb.com/title/tt0078788/, directed by Francis Ford Coppola, (1979, Beverly Hills CA: United Artists).
[32] Thomas Stearns Eliot, The Waste Land (New York: Horace Liveright, 1922).
[33] Frazer op cit and Joseph Conrad, The Heart of Darkness (New York: Penguin, 1999).
[34] Jessie Laidlay Weston, From Ritual to Romance (Cambridge: Cambridge University Press, 1920).

theory" if you like, detailed and painstaking local history and the
contextual shift in North American folkloristics described above. Thus, by
the time I sat in a cinema to watch *Apocalypse Now* as a second year PhD
student, that shot of the bookshelf was for me as significant as anything in
the film. Willard wasn't just killing off Kurtz but an entire scholarly
project. Yet none of this detracted from my response to traditional
performance. By 1979 I knew that the works that had represented my first
real engagement with the world of ideas, works that had provided
architecture for my emotional and embodied responses to the idea of ritual
in performance, and the way in which I was drawn to the traditional in
performance, intellectually at least, were built on the sand of mid and late-
Victorian and Edwardian fashion. Conversely, my work on mumming had
made me part of the tradition of anthropological fieldwork, which then
took me to south western Ethiopia and engagement with dramatic
elements of traditional ceremonies, and I still couldn't shake the romance
of repetition and ritual from my interest in the customary. In one way or
another I had not succumbed to the twin lures of survivalism and the
exotic: I had sprinted headlong towards them.

Lastly, when I started to perform in a mummers' play in 1971, when I
began to study mummers' plays in earnest in 1976, I had never heard of
French critical theory. I knew nothing of Deleuze, Derrida, or Foucault,
but today I can't separate what I think about these apparently simple
performances from some of those (less apparently) complex ideas. Like
the performances themselves they have become part of my conceptual
topography. The meanings I construct are perpetually shifting, they're not
fixed, they can't derive entirely from the performance tradition that so
engages me. So while I am definitely drawn to the fixity of tradition I'm
also absolutely secure in the knowledge that what comes later will be
different. And here we go: Derrida and différance: "to defer" and "to
differ" where Derrida's coinage plays on the fact that the words are
homophonous in French and in the world, because whatever comes later
will be different. I particularly like an 1834 definition of ethnography in
this context, "the customs, habits and differences of races of man,"[35]
because it allows a further reconsideration of difference and différance
since that which is customary and habitual (and invariably local) is not just
indicative of difference, but of deferral. The repeated—and the customary
and habitual are by definition repeated—must always and increasingly

---

[35] *The Shorter Oxford English Dictionary*, vol 1., eds. William Little, H. W.
Fowler and Jessie Coulson (Oxford: Oxford University Press, 1983), s.v.,
"Ethnography."

defer from the original action. And as for Deleuze? How could it be possible to consider folklore "now" without acknowledging the content of his arguably most famous title *Difference and Repetition*?[36] And Deleuze, of course, was a friend of Foucault, whose work on discourse, and crucially his noting of the leakage of discourse, will always critique my unsatisfactory efforts at synthesis across the discourses of drama, folklore, ethnography, anthropology and critical theory.

Soulcaking[37]

I'll begin to move towards mumming now, to engage with a more specific exploration of the gaps between frames of reference on the one hand, and the particularities of tradition and performance on the other. We have to acknowledge that there are often gaps between the known history of particular mumming performances, the not-so-known histories of the source material, and the fuzzy-geography of the constructed meta-tradition in which performers and audiences can choose to place their action. Indeed the study of mummers' plays and the efforts to plug those information gaps through the multiple frames of reference just outlined might be regarded as an enduring popular entertainment in its own right. This was recognised by Mat Levitt in 2010, in an MA dissertation submitted to the Department of Anthropology at the University of Alberta:

> There are a great number of stories told about the English folk play tradition known as "mummers" plays'. These stories told by folklorists, historians, anthropologists, popular fiction writers, mummers and audience members, and lay folk in general, can be considered as part of a body of folk commentary or metafolklore. Within this body of metafolklore, there are, generally speaking, at least five types of narratives told to explain the

---

[36] Gilles Deleuze, Difference and Repetition (London: Athlone Press, 1994).

[37] Soulcaking is a regional form of mumming specific to North West England. Refer to http://www.mastermummers.org/ . For detailed description and discussion of the specific Antrobus play on which my subsequent points rest see Anthony Green, "Popular Drama and the Mummers' Play," in Performance and Politics in Popular Drama, ed. David Bradby, Louis James and Bernard Sharratt (Cambridge: Cambridge University Press, 1980), 139-166; Peter Harrop, "The Performance of English Folk Plays: A Study in Dramatic Form and Social Function" (PhD diss., University of Leeds, 1980); Susan Pattison, "The Antrobus Soulcaking Play: An Alternative Approach to the Mummers' Play," Folk Life: A Journal of Ethnological Studies 15, (1977): 5-11. Soulcaking at Antrobus, Brotherton Library Special Collections, LAVC/FIL/F005 University of Leeds: 1975. The Antrobus Soulcakers, Garland Films. 2009.

origins of the tradition [...] it is possible to trace, if not the origin, then the development of each of the origin stories told about the tradition [...] through space and time but [also] across lines of scholarship, literary fiction and folk commentary [...] perhaps scholarship and literature can be considered as part of the body of metafolklore; as constituents rather than objective observer.[38]

If we take Levin's advice we may start to find the performance of informed spectatorship as a consequence of ethnographic engagement, a demonstrably embodied and performative engagement.

I first turned up in the village of Antrobus in Cheshire with a camera and a portable reel to reel tape recorder during the evening of October 31st 1977. Going back to my earlier definition of ethnography the custom, habit and difference I went looking for in Antrobus was the Soulcaking Gang and its Soulcaking Play, a short performance about strangers, fighting and killing, coming back to life, cross dressing, charlatans, tramps, simpletons, and the keeping of a horse's skull. The play is customary and habitual, performed in and around the Cheshire village of Antrobus some 25 times each year between Halloween and mid-November. Soulcaking starts each year on All Souls Eve and runs into mid-November. Soul cake is a regional name given to shortbread flavoured with cinnamon, but the Antrobus Soulcakers do not distribute soul cake. They perform a play. Nine men arrive outside a pub. The current complement includes a father and two sons, two brothers, and four cousins. Five of them are Antrobus born and bred and remain residents. The others have either lived in Antrobus or are from close by. They sing a song announcing their arrival which people in the pub may or may not hear. One of them raps on the door with a cane and walks in, a well-dressed man in top hat and tails, announcing that there will be a "dreadful fight." A soldier in nineteenth-century military uniform comes in claiming to be the Black Prince and boasting of his prowess. A second soldier, King George, refutes his claims and engages him in combat. The Black Prince is slain; his distraught mother arrives and calls for a doctor. A quack arrives and brings him back to life. The odd but harmless Dairy Doubt appears, introduces himself and exits. The tramp Beelzebub enters, steals beer and drinks it, and exits. A horse (actually a man beneath a cover holding a real horse's skull on a stake, thus conveying the appearance of a three legged horse) careers in through the onlookers. The horse has a companion called

---

[38] Mat J. Levitt, "The Laughing Storyteller: Metafolklore about the origins of Mummers." (MA diss., University of Alberta, 2011), Abstract.

"the driver" who speaks on his behalf. The gang sing a concluding song, collect money and move on to the next performance. The performers arrive, perform, and leave each venue in the space of about thirty minutes before travelling to their next location.

Soulcaking is very local, but part of a much bigger picture, and I find it intriguing that many of the performance principles utilised by Soulcakers will be familiar to those exploring site specific performance and pursuing the "mobility turn" in contemporary performance. I pointed out recently that the interplay of site specificity and mobility is commonplace in traditional performance, usually as a perambulation between pre-determined sites. Furthermore, repetition, return and retracing by performers and audiences, often over extended periods of many years, are the defining features of calendar customs. This enables a different conceptualisation of duration and mobility to that informing much contemporary performance, and allows for the development of a special relationship between people, site and memory. In Alain Badiou's words, "it happens that something happens. That something happens to us."[39] Our acts of repeated re-visiting may be a collective searching out of these personal singularities. I'd like to quote here from a recent article in which I tried to summarise what I think is going on at Antrobus, and because I want to try and tease out two broader points:

> In my view the repetition that makes tradition is channelled, harnessed and celebrated because it is, as is all performance, in Diana Taylor's phrase "a system of learning, storing and transmitting knowledge" […] When asked of Soulcaking at Antrobus "who's it for?" Ian McCormack, one of the performers, responds that "you're doing it to do it." But in the act of "being done to be done," traditional performance is using site and time, repetition and return, to construct a portal where the "here" of place and "when" of calendar can intersect. We put ourselves in a place where the present can be invaded by shafts of involuntary and unexpected memory. I suggest this underpins the efficacy and popularity of calendar customs.[40]

The performer Ian McCormack first performed with the Soulcakers the year I commenced my fieldwork. His understanding and feel for the tradition is inextricably connected to the duration of his engagement, and my understanding of that is premised on mine. The fact that I have also engaged with a calendar custom in a home place means I share a sense of

---

[39] Alain Badiou, On Beckett, Trans. Nina Power and Alberto Toscano, (Manchester: Clinamen Press, 2003), 77.
[40] Harrop, "The Antrobus Soulcakers," 273.

what it is to return and re-trace and to play with palimpsest and pentimento both as performer and spectator. It is this, simply, that affords me any insight I may have. My second point is that the insights thus gained may have wider and broader application despite the very singular conditions in which they were formed. I think that may be one value of ethnography.

To conclude, our chapters look for ways to look critically at those moments of music/dance/drama performance, those deeply engaging moments of ethnographic encounter; moments of dilemma and insecurity, often outside the comfort zone of scholarly methodologies, but nevertheless inherent to practice-based research. (And "it happens that something happens. That something happens to us.")[41] These moments contain what Jon McKenzie calls the "multiplicity of forces"[42] of performance studies as they connect and re-connect disparate fields of social interactions. In revisiting the territory of the performance orientation, in touching on anthropology, dance, folklore, music and theatre to look for present trends in the ethnography of performance (and performance ethnography is one of those trends) I see three related endeavours. One: an embodied, affective and sensory ethnography that privileges encounters between ethnographer, participants and practices as key to understanding and knowledge. Two: individuals shaped by their engagement with ethnographic practice in the midst of the migration, diffusion, revival, appropriation and commodification of performance. Three: the interface of academic disciplines with the idea of performance, and the ways in which academics and practitioners are drawn to ethnography to better understand, negotiate, perform and profess their diverse fields.

Works Cited

Apocalypse Now. IMDb www.imdb.com/title/tt0078788/. Directed by Francis Ford Coppola. 1979; Beverly Hills CA: United Artists.

Atkinson, Paul. "Performing Ethnography and the Ethnography of Performance." *British Journal of Sociology of Education* 25, Issue 1, (2004): 107-114.

Badiou, Allan. *On Beckett*. Trans. Nina Power and Alberto Toscano. Manchester: Clinamen Press, 2003.

---

[41] Badiou, *On Beckett.*
[42] Jon McKenzie, Perform or Else: From Discipline to Performance (London: Routledge, 2001).

Bauman, Richard. "Introduction." In *Toward New Perspectives in Folklore*, edited by Americo Paredes and Richard Bauman, v-ix. Austin: American Folklore Society, 1971.

Ben-Amos, Dan, and Kenneth S. Goldstein, eds. "Introduction." In *Folklore: Performance and Communication Issue 40 of Approaches to Semiotics*, 2-10. The Hague: Mouton & Co., 1975.

Brody, Alan. *The English Mummers and their Plays: Traces of Ancient Mystery*. London: Routledge and Kegan Paul, 1969.

Buckland, Theresa. "English Folk Dance Scholarship: A Review," In *Traditional Dance,* vol. 1., edited by Theresa Buckland. Crewe and Alsager College, 1982.

Carlson, Marvin. *Performance: A Critical Introduction*. London: Routledge, 1996.

Cawte Chrostopher, Alex Helm and Norman Peacock. *English Ritual Drama: A Geographical Index*. London: The Folk-Lore Society, 1977.

Conrad, Joseph. *The Heart of Darkness*. New York: Penguin, 1999.

Deleuze, Gilles. *Difference and Repetition*. London: Athlone Press, 1994.

Green, Anthony. "Popular Drama and the Mummers' Play." In *Performance and Politics in Popular Drama*, edited by David Bradby, Louis James and Bernard Sharratt, 139-166. Cambridge: Cambridge University Press, 1980.

Denzin, Norman K. *Performance Ethnography: Critical Pedagogy and the Politics of Culture*. Thousand Oaks; London; New Delhi: Sage Publications, 2003.

Dorson, Richard M. "Current Folklore Theories." *Current Anthropology* 4, (1963): 93-112.

—. ed., *Folklore and Folklife: An Introduction*. Chicago: University of Chicago Press, 1972.

—. *The British Folklorists: A History*. London: Routledge and Kegan Paul, 1968.

—. *Peasant Customs and Savage Myths: Selections from the British Folklorists*, 2 vols. Chicago and London: University of Chicago Press, Routledge and Kegan Paul, 1968.

Eliot, Thomas Stearns. *The Waste Land.* New York: Horace Liveright, 1922.

Glassie, Henry. *All Silver and no Brass: An Irish Christmas Mumming*. Indiana: Indiana University Press, 1975.

Frazer, James G. *The Golden Bough, A Study in Comparative Religion*, 2 vols. London: Macmillan, 1894.

Halpert, Herbert, and G.M. Story. eds. *Christmas Mumming in Newfoundland*. Toronto: University of Toronto Press, 1969.

Harrop, Peter. "The Performance of English Folk Plays: A Study in Dramatic Form and Social Function." PhD diss., University of Leeds, 1980.

—. "What's in a Name? A Comparison of UK and US Performance Studies." *Studies in Theatre and Performance* 25, no. 3 (2005): 189-201.

—. "The Antrobus Soulcakers: A consideration of site, mobility and time as components of traditional performance." *Contemporary Theatre Review* 22, no. 2 (2012): 267-273.

Hymes, Dell. "Breakthrough into Performance." In *Folklore: Performance and Communication Issue 40 of Approaches to Semiotics*, edited by Dan Ben-Amos and Kenneth S. Goldstein, 11-74. The Hague: Mouton & Co., 1975.

Jackson, Shannon. *Professing Performance: Theatre in the Academy from Philology to Performativity*. Cambridge: Cambridge University Press, 2004.

Knowles, Ric. *Theatre and Interculturalism*. Basingstoke: Palgrave Macmillan, 2010.

Levitt, Mat J. "The Laughing Storyteller: Metafolklore about the origins of Mummers." MA diss., University of Alberta, 2011.

Magnat, Virginie. "Can Research Become Ceremony? Performance Ethnography and Indigenous Epistemologies." *Canadian Theatre Review* 151, (2012): 30-36.

McKenzie, Jon. *Perform or Else: From Discipline to Performance*. London: Routledge, 2001.

Master Mummers. "Master Mummers" http://www.mastermummers.org/.

Paredes, Americo, and Richard Bauman, eds. "Special Edition: Towards New Perspectives in Folklore." *Journal of American Folklore* 84, (1971).

—. "Foreword." In *Toward New Perspectives in Folklore*, edited by Americo Paredes and Richard Bauman, iii-iv. Austin: American Folklore Society, 1971.

Pattison, Susan. "The Antrobus Soulcaking Play: An Alternative Approach to the Mummers' Play." *Folk Life: A Journal of Ethnological Studies* 15, (1977): 5-11.

Pollock, Della. "Marking New Directions in Performance Ethnography." *Text and Performance Quarterly* 26, issue 4 (2006): 325-329.

Roms, Heike. "The Practice Turn: Performance and the British Academy." In *Contesting Performance: Global Sites of Research*, edited by Jon McKenzie, Heike Roms and C.J.W.-L. Wee, 51-70. London: Palgrave Macmillan, 2010.

Rusted, Brian. "Introduction: From Ethnography of Performance to Performance Ethnography." *Canadian Theatre Review* 151, (2012): 3-6.

Schechner, Richard. *Between Theater and Anthropology*. Philadelphia: University of Pennsylvania Press, 1985.

Sharp, Cecil J. *The Sword Dances of Northern England*. East Ardsley: E.P. Publishing, 1977.

Smith, Paul, and J.D.A. Widdowson. "Traditional Drama Studies." *Traditional Drama* vol. 1, Centre for English Cultural Tradition and Language and the Traditional Drama Research Group, edited by Paul Smith and J.D.A Widdowson. Doncaster: January Books, 1985.

Soulcaking at Antrobus, Brotherton Library Special Collections, LAVC/FIL/F005 University of Leeds: 1975.

The Antrobus Soulcakers, Garland Films, 2009.

The Traditional Drama Research Group. "The Folk Play" The Traditional Drama Research Group, http://www.folkplay.info/.

Tyler, Edward B. *Primitive Culture, Researches into the Development of Mythology, Philosophy, Religion, Art and Custom*, 2 vols., London: J. Murray, 1871.

Warren, John. "Introduction: Performance Ethnography: A TPQ Symposium." *Text and Performance Quarterly* 26, Issue 4 (2006): 317-319.

Weston, Jessie Laidlay. *From Ritual to Romance*. Cambridge: Cambridge University Press, 1920.

CHAPTER TWO

PERFORMANCE ETHNOGRAPHY: THEATRE AND ANTHROPOLOGY THROUGH THE NEW STUDY OF RITUAL

DUNJA NJARADI

> [P]erformance has much in common with the enterprise of ethnography
> [...] Both are framed activities, concerned with giving meaning to
> experience [...].
> —Deborah Kapchan[1]

> Whether practitioners and scholars of either discipline like it or not, there
> are points of contact between anthropology and theatre; and there are likely
> to be more coming.
> —Richard Schechner[2]

The intention of this chapter is to broadly discuss some theoretical and methodological ground for performance ethnography. As anthropologist Deborah Kapchan noted in the epigraph above to truly understand performance one is likely to stumble upon the epistemological baggage of ethnography. This is only logical since from the beginning performance (studies) is the outcome of a brief but fruitful encounter between anthropology and theatre. Here I am referring to "theatre anthropology," an interdisciplinary collaboration between Victor Turner and Richard Schechner. This collaboration initiated some significant shifts in theatre studies, anthropology, and also across wider social sciences, arts and humanities. The article is divided into several parts that trace and reflect these shifts in different disciplines—anthropology, dance studies, performance and theatre studies. Further, in the spirit of Schechner's prediction above

---

[1] Deborah Kapchan, "Performance," The Journal of American Folklore 108, no. 430 (1995): 483.
[2] Richard Schechner, Between Theater and Anthropology (Philadelphia: University of Philadelphia Press, 1985), 3.

on the *future* points of contact between theatre and anthropology, the article discusses some recent theories of magic (and) ritual in anthropology. In other words, I wish to outline the possibility of "theatre anthropology" or "performance anthropology" for the twenty-first century. To do this, I will turn my attention to the ritual as a site of initial Schechner-Turner contact. In his publication *The Future of the Ritual* where he revisited some of his first collaborative moments with Turner, Schechner states that "[e]ven to say it in one word, ritual, is asking for trouble."[3] He is referring to the messy concept of the ritual being simultaneously explained as the 'oldest' behaviour rooted in what 'reptiles' do; inherent to the 'old' cultures—something that 'natives' do; [and as] a repository of higher symbols and religion."[4] I won't try to untangle and clarify this messy web, rather I intend to discuss the event of ritual performance seen through the eyes of an anthropologist looking through the lenses of performance studies, thus reconnecting performance and anthropology. A second, minor framework, will consider anthropological difficulties with magic as something that constantly escapes and eludes scientific/rational explanation as a positive way of rethinking and reconnecting anthropology and performance studies. Concluding remarks will return to performance ethnography and the "transformative vitality"[5] of ethnographic and performance practices.

Theatre Anthropology

   This section will revisit a collaboration that heralded huge theoretical and methodological shift in Arts and Humanities in the late 20th century— I am referring here to "theatre anthropology"[6]or the "drama analogy"[7] as euphemism for a most fruitful interdisciplinary collaboration between anthropologist Victor Turner and theatre practitioner Richard Schechner. The collaboration between Turner and Schechner resulted in Turner's *From Ritual to Theatre* (1982) and Schechner's *Between Theater and Anthropology* (1985). The strongest point of contact between theatre and anthropology in the Turner/Schechner dialogue was the study of ritual. According to Turner, a ritual is the most powerful active genre of cultural

---

[3] Richard Schechner, The Future of the Ritual: Writings on Culture and Performance (London and New York: Routledge, 1995), 228.
[4] Ibid., 251
[5] Brian Rusted, "Editor's note" Canadian Theatre Review 151, (2012).
[6] Eugenio Barba, "Theatre Anthropology," The Drama Review 94, no. 2 (1982): 5-32.
[7] Clifford Geertz, "Blurred Genres," American Scholar 49, no. 2 (1980): 165-182.

performance. Following the work of an early twentieth-century Belgian anthropologist Arnold Van Gennep, Turner explains how the process by which one individual changes his/her social status in a performative way can be called "liminal process." Turner is responsible for the affirmation and dissemination of Van Gennep's structure of ritual especially the rituals that mark the transitional stages in man's life or "the rites of passage." Van Gennep asserts that all the transitional rituals (birth, puberty, marriage, death) have the same structure consisting of three phases: pre-liminal (separation), liminal (in-between stage) and post-liminal (incorporation). Turner, for the most part, focused his study on the middle phase which he deemed ambivalent, powerful and dangerous. Liminal stages can generally be found in the rituals of pre-industrial societies as they are compulsory outcomes of the collective inspiration. In post-industrial Western societies Turner identifies *liminoid* practices which are purely elective and the result of individual agency. As Turner asserts: "One *works* at the liminal, one *plays* at the liminoid."[8] Schechner was particularly inspired by Turner's study of ritual to tease out the connections between ritual behavior and theatrical (re)production. He uses Turner's schema of the structure of ritual, and especially liminal/liminoid distinctions, to apply it to performance behaviour:

A performance involves a separation, a transition, and an incorporation [...] In initiations people are transformed permanently whereas in most performances the transformations are temporary (transportations). Like initiations, performances "make" one person into another. Unlike initiation, performances usually see to it that the performer gets his own self back. To use Van Gennep's categories, training, workshop, rehearsal, and warm-ups are preliminary rites of separation. The performance itself is liminal, analogous to the rites of transition. Cool-down and aftermath are postliminal, rites of incorporation.[9]

Further to this, Schechner sees the potential in theatre/anthropology collaboration in the transmission of performance knowledge. Anthropologists as "trained observers" can help theatre practitioners to see performances as part of specific socio-cultural systems. Theatre practitioners, on the other hand, with extensive performance training, can help anthropologists in analysing a particular performance situation.[10] Expanding the definition of

---

[8] Victor Turner, From Ritual to Theatre: the human seriousness of play (New York: PAJ Publications, 1982), 55.
[9] Schechner, *Between Theater*, 20-21.
[10] Ibid., 25.

performance to include performative behaviour in everyday life, ritual, aesthetic dance and theatre, initiation rites, sport events and psychoanalysis, Turner helped Schechner pave the way to creating a new discipline, Performance Studies, which will be discussed in the following section.

Performance Studies

By connecting theatre and anthropology Turner and Schechner raised some fundamental questions related to cultural behavior. Despite cultural diversity, they conclude, all cultures display a curious tendency towards theatricality which means that performance is a universal and transcultural mode of communication. Thus Schechner's definition of performance event and its wide application had a significant impact across disciplines and his collaboration with Turner, usually referred to as the "performance turn," not only brought about massive shifts in anthropology, sociology, and folkloristics, but is also generative of performance studies, a discipline whose links (and working relationship) with theatre and drama are still debatable[11] and whose boundaries are still unclear. Nevertheless, Performance Studies has a major place in Arts and Humanities as the "performance paradigm" still operates as a major theoretical and analytical concept. To emphasise the importance of performance studies Jon McKenzie claims that performance is "the power matrix of contemporary globalization" and continues that "[t]oday, all cultures, all organizations, all technical systems can be studied in terms of different, yet historically related, performance paradigms."[12] In relation to particular disciplines, this performance paradigm brought a "shift in emphasis from the playscript to the actor's body; in dance attention moved from formal choreography to movements of everyday life [...] in anthropology ethnographers shifted their attention from mystic structures to their embodiment in rituals."[13] In folklore studies, the influence of the performance paradigm was equally compelling. Richard Bauman, for instance, emphasised that in folklore research "the term 'performance' has been used to convey a dual sense of artistic *action*—doing of folklore—and artistic event—the performance situation, involving performer, art form, audience and settings—both of

---

[11] Roberta Mock and Ruth Way, "Pedagogies of Theatre (Arts) and Performance (Studies)," Studies in Theatre and Performance 25, no. 3 (2005): 201-213.
[12] Jon McKenzie, "Democracy's Performance," The Drama Review 47, no. 2 (2003): 118.
[13] Jon McKenzie, Perform or Else: From Discipline to Performance (New York: Routledge, 2001), 37.

which are basic to the developing performance approach."[14] In general then, we can conclude that the performance paradigm really "turned the tables" in re-orientating anthropological research towards the moment and context of performance rather than deep underlying social and psychological structures. Turner's orientation in performance analysis also shifted attention to the body in ritual analysis. In Pnina Werbner's words: "[…] Victor Turner's study of the Ndembu ritual has been foundational in revealing the rootedness of ethical ideas in the body and body substances, manipulated and worked upon to achieve a social, emotional and moral transformation of a liminal subject."[15]

The universalism and transculturalism implied in theatre anthropology received some harsh criticism with a postmodern turn in anthropology. From the literary turn of the 1980's, the realist practices of representation in ethnography are challenged by what Marcus termed "messy texts" (1986) which presuppose "partial and fluid epistemological and cultural assumptions, fragmented writing styles, and troubled notions of ethnographic legitimacy [...]."[16] This provocative challenge was set out in the collective essays *Writing Culture* which represented a schism in ethnographic research—the process of writing ethnographies was problematised with a profound self-consciousness about the power relations inherent in the representation of the Other. With the ethnographic "real" being problematised and profoundly questioned, ethnographers of today are those who "both know too much and know too little."[17] In the light of these changes, theatre anthropology was charged to be a new form of Western imperialism that sought to uproot cultural forms from their cultural contexts and commodify them for the Western consumer.[18] However, the influence of theatre anthropology exemplified in the rise of performance studies and especially the individual work of Turner and

---

[14] Richard Bauman, *Verbal Art as Performance* (Rowley Mass., 1977), vii, quoted in Simon J. Bronner, "Art, Performance, and Praxis: the Rhetoric of Contemporary Folklore Studies," Western Folklore 47, no. 2 (1988): 87.

[15] Pnina Werbner and Helene Basu, "The Embodiment of Charisma," in Embodying Charisma: Modernity, Locality, and the Performance of Emotion in Sufi Cults, ed. Phina Werbner and Helene Basu (Manchester: Manchester University Press, 1998), 7.

[16] Patti Lather, "Working the Ruins of Feminist Ethnography," Signs 27, no. 1 (2001): 201.

[17] Ibid., 302.

[18] see Ian Watson, Negotiating Cultures: Eugenio Barba and the Intercultural Debate (Manchester: Manchester University Press, 2002), 23-30.

Schechner seems to have survived post-modern criticism—perhaps not entirely intact but certainly not entirely discredited. For instance, although usually considered functionalist and structuralist, Graham St John sees Turner as "a genuinely transitional figure working in a significant period of colonial/ethnographic change [and] it appears that Turner occupied the threshold between modern and postmodern thought."[19] Although Turner himself developed a structural schema for ritual (which relied on an expanded version of Van Gennep's ritual theory) in *The Forest of Symbols* he went on to introduce a valuable caveat:

> Anthropologists are still vitally concerned to exhibit "structures" and social relations, ideas, and values, but they now tend to see these in relation to processes of which they are both the products and regulators. Process-theory involves "becoming" as well as a "being" vocabulary [...].[20]

Finally Turner concludes: "[...] I prefer to regard transition as a process, a becoming, and in the case of rites de passage even a transformation [...]."[21] Turner's insistence that Ndembu rituals are not only disguises of deeper social and psychological processes, but have ontological value, prompted Bruce Kapferer to state that "Turner was directed to ritual as process in the more philosophical meaning of becoming,"[22] and he believed that the "ritual practices *as themselves* already include their theoretical possibility."[23] I will came back to later to Kapferer's re-conceptualisation of ritual, at present I wish to emphasize how Turner's pivotal concept of limen (liminality) has been taken and reworked by performance studies scholars and philosophers from Deleuze and Guattari's "becoming theories" to Jon McKenzie's "reconfiguring liminality in the digital age."[24]

---

[19] Graham St John, "An Introduction," in Victor Turner and Contemporary Cultural Performance, ed. Graham St John (New York: Berghahn Books, 2008), 12.
[20] Victor Turner, The Forest of Symbols: Aspects of Ndembu Ritual (New York and London: Cornell University Press, 1970), 112-113.
[21] Ibid., 94.
[22] Bruce Kapferer, "Ritual Dynamics and Virtual Practice: Beyond Representation and Meaning," in Ritual in its own right: Exploring the Dynamics of Transformation, ed. Don Handelman and Galina Lindquist, 35-55 (New York: Berghahn Books, 2004).
[23] Ibid., 38, emphasis added.
[24] See McKenzie, *Perform or Else.*

Take for instance theatre scholar Jill Dolan who draws heavily from Turner's concept of communitas and social drama when theorising utopian performance. She discusses utopian performativity as a transformative property of *live* performance. Following Turner's writing on communitas, Dolan understands utopian performativity as a deep style of personal interaction that "has something magical about it."[25] However, Dolan fails to distinguish between liminal phenomena—where the permanent transformation inherent to ritual performance occurs—and the liminoid phenomena of artistic (theatrical) performance. This example is one of many that prompted Graham St John to point out a paradox of performance studies scholarship:

> Critical scrutiny of Turner's work demonstrates how, not long after his death, the academy would develop an institutional mistrust of transcendent principles and universal absolutes, triggering a decommissioning of essentialism. Yet, as Jon McKenzie conveys […], poststructuralism provided a platform for the (re)invigoration of what Phillip Auslander […] identified as the "transgressive" or "resistant" theme inscribed in liminality —an approach said to have constituted something of a "liminal-norm" in performance studies (thus often denying the either/or pivot central to Turner's thesis).[26]

Thus Performance Studies, although carrying certain re-worked anthropological heritage, lost its connection with anthropology and found its theoretical, methodological, and institutional backing in the plethora of theories (cultural studies, gender and queer studies, postcolonial studies, and so on) that made a significant impact on social sciences and humanities during the 1980's. Something similar has occurred in the field of dance studies which will be discussed in the next section.

Dance Studies

Dance anthropologist Theresa Buckland notes that during the second part of the twentieth-century studies of dance show a tendency towards dissociating from anthropology and aligning with cultural studies where dance is more likely to be seen as a text of culture. Buckland claims that:

> [m]ost of the dance studies literature based on the notion of dance as cultural production does not derive its theoretical base directly from anthropology, for which the relativity of cultures has been a conceptual

---

[25] Ibid., 473.
[26] St John, 16.

cornerstone [...] Instead this dance literature draws variously upon gender and cultural studies, critical theory and performance studies, disciplines that do not share the same aims and histories [as] anthropology. [27]

This created a certain developmental trend in dance research. The dance anthropologist Brenda Farnell, for instance, in her *Ethnography and the Moving Body*, argues that there is a fundamental problem with Western ways of viewing human movement. She suggests that despite an upsurge of interest in "the body," an understanding of a person as a moving agent is still absent from cultural theory and ethnographic accounts.[28] Jane Desmond also traces this "turn to the body" in the social sciences with the advent of cultural studies, concluding, much in line with Farnell, that this critical work focused on the representation of the body rather than on bodily movement/actions. To Desmond this "academy's aversion to the material body, and its fictive separation of mental and physical production, has rendered humanities scholarship that investigates the mute dancing body nearly invisible." [29]

Buckland notices how this association with cultural studies quickly built up two major "myths" in dance studies and dance anthropology. The first myth presupposes that anthropology of dance means applying theories of culture on dance and the dancing body or viewing dances and bodies as "texts." The second "myth" stems from the colonial history of the discipline—Buckland notices how dance research tended to privilege the investigation of "exotic" cultures over the consideration of the dance practices of high and popular cultures of Western Europe and America. It is interesting to note how this tendency differs from the tradition of Eastern European folkloristics and ethnochoreology. Lacking in colonial experience, Eastern European folkloristics turned to their own "peasant societies" which were deemed privileged carriers of ethno-national sentiments. Coming from a similar perspective to Buckland, dance anthropologist Deidre Sklar also notes how the influence of cultural studies has been exceptionally strong in dance studies when assessing the situation in the North-American scholarship. Sklar identifies this trajectory

---

[27] Theresa Buckland, "All Dances are Ethnic but Some Are More Ethnic than Others: Some Observations on Dance Studies and Anthropology," Dance Research Journal 17, no. 1 (1999):4.

[28] Brenda Farnell, "Ethno-Graphic and the moving body," Man, New Series 29 (1994): 929-974.

[29] Jane Desmond, "Terra Incognita: Mapping New Territory in Dance and 'Cultural Studies,'" Dance Research Journal 32, no. 1 (2000): 34.

as socio-political and she names authors like Susan Foster, whose post-structuralist approach is through theories of the body and the way bodies produce and signify individual, gender, ethnic, and group identities. Sklar concludes that this "socio-cultural" trajectory of dance studies developed its theoretical grounds from a literature external to dance. On the opposite side of the spectrum Sklar identifies "kinesthetic trajectory" as having a special bearing on dance anthropology as it "grew internally, out of dance methodology."[30] This trajectory pays more attention to movement than to the body and the ways through which movement itself can communicate meanings in an immediate somatic way. Sally Ann Ness and Cynthia Novack are dance anthropologists whose studies in the 1990's drew broader attention to the ways in which kinesthetic, felt knowledge may be incorporated in more conventional ethnographies. Both ethnographers relied on their own sense of movement when conducting ethnography. Participation in dances they observed was pivotal, not merely to gain a better, "thicker" description of movements and choreographies but "to understand the way sensation itself is organized, in the dancing certainly, and also, in Ness's words, as 'latent symbolism' of social action." [31] This approach to kinesthetic empathy has been critiqued in Susan Foster's 2011 book *Choreographing Empathy: Kinesthesia in Performance.*[32] Indeed, Sklar herself admits that the kinesthetic trajectory still struggles to find ways of translating somatic knowledge into texts—still the biggest challenge for dance if not performance ethnography in general.

Finally, Sklar provides an example from her own fieldwork to illustrate the claim that the ethnographer's *physical* experience of fieldwork must have a pivotal role in his/her ethnography. When describing preparations for the celebratory fiesta in honour of the virgin of Guadalupe in Tortugas, New Mexico, Sklar reflects on changing sensations of time/space that the practice of ritual preparation provided:

> The actions of the fiesta—dusting the vigas, chopping onions, dancing, walking in the procession—created not just the synchronized rhythms of people habituated to working together, but the transformation of attention. That attention was both diffused and focused. In it, time was roomy so that impressions and ideas slowed and sharpened. [...] Imperceptibly, I had learned to recognize and step into this quality of time. "Tell them this is

---

[30] Deidre Sklar, "On Dance Ethnography," Dance Research Journal 32, no. 1 (2000): 70.
[31] Ibid., 71.
[32] Susan Foster, Choreographing Empathy: Kinesthesia in Performance (London: Routledge, 2011).

how we clean," the mother of two young women once instructed me, as a joke. But the joke named a truth: the fiesta's transformation capacity lay in details of work. If I could indeed tell how they cleaned, I would be showing how the fiesta achieved its effect. Spiritual knowledge, the feeling of the virgin's presence, came as a *doing*, transformation enacted upon oneself through the details of work. [33]

This passage was worth quoting at length not only because it documents an "inside" of the fieldwork experience but also because, unwittingly, it provides a strong claim on the nature of ritual/performance *per se*: an emphasis on "practice" or "doing;" an idea of transformation of the quality of time through a particular organisation of sensation. This form of engagement with ritual is being developed in more recent studies of ritual, where ritual has come to be seen not (only) as a choreographed outcome of a particular cultural notion but as an event in itself—not confined to the logic of cultural expression but, unsurprisingly, as "reality *in* its own."[34] Correspondingly, Beeman when writing about performance in general finds it very problematic that

> [a]nthropologists have studied performance largely for what it can show about other human institutions such as religion, political life, gender relations, and ethnic identity. Less study has been devoted to the performance per se: its structure, its cultural meaning apart from other institutions, the conditions under which it occurs, and its place within broad patterns of community life. [35]

Sklar's role as *dance* anthropologist seems to set out to address this lack in anthropological scholarship. However, her account is noteworthy and useful for the study of ritual as it calls for the close observation of the ritual *per se* the way it is "put together and organized within itself"[36] —or ritual in its own right. The next section will turn to anthropology and recent studies of magic and ritual to finally discuss the possible new connections between performance and anthropology that may serve for the future.

---

[33] Sklar, 71-2.

[34] Bruce Kapferer, The Feast of the Sorcerer: Practices of Consciousness and Power (Chicago: University of Chicago Press, 1997); see also Don Handelman, "Why Ritual in its own right?" in Ritual in its own right: Exploring the Dynamics of Transformation, ed. Don Handelman and Galina Lindquist, 1-35 (New York: Berghahn Books, 2004). Emphasis added.

[35] William O. Beeman, "The Anthropology of Theater and Spectacle," Annual Review of Anthropology 22, (1993): 370.

[36] Handelman, "Why Ritual in its own right?," 2.

Anthropology

Anthropologists are merchants of the strange.
—Clifford Geertz[37]

Bruce Kapferer in the introduction to his *Beyond Rationalism: Rethinking Magic, Witchcraft, and Sorcery* claims that magic, together with sorcery and witchcraft, is at the epistemological centre of anthropology. According to Kapferer the questions that these phenomena raise "are of enduring significance for the discipline"[38] because they "[p]oint to matters of deep existential concerns in a general quest for understanding of the human forces engaged in the human construction of lived realities."[39] Kapferer's provocative suggestion is that the question of magic, witchcraft and sorcery lies at the heart of the discipline as they challenge the epistemological boundaries of anthropology itself—the features of reason and "unreason" in the human psyche, the foundations of religion and the very nature of science.[40]

Kapferer's writings on magic are closely connected with his understanding of ritual to a degree that magic does not exist without a set of embodied techniques and activities which are always immanent and emergent and never or rarely abstract. This idea of ritual as practice comes from postmodern anthropologists and performance scholars who suggested that "[t]hose mysterious rituals that aroused such intense admiration and curiosity among earlier observers, […] should be seen not as expressions of some distinctive essence but simply as a different kind of practice."[41] However, Kapferer draws his conclusions on magic as *practice and performance* from Evans-Pritchard's pioneering work on Zande magic thus revealing this strand of thought in early ethnographies of magic as well. The other important early disciplinary cornerstone of Kapferer's ideas is Marcel Mauss's pioneering work on techniques of the body. As

---

[37] Quoted in Bruce Kapferer, "Introduction: Outside All Reason: Magic, Sorcery, and Epistemology in Anthropology," in Beyond Rationalism: Rethinking Magic, Witchcraft and Sorcery, ed. Bruce Kapferer (New York: Berghahn Books, 2002), 2.
[38] Ibid., 1.
[39] Ibid.
[40] Ibid., 11.
[41] Jeffrey C. Alexander, "Cultural Pragmatics: Social Performance between ritual and strategy," Sociological Theory 22, no. 4 (2004): 534.

early as 1922 Marcel Mauss had claimed that body techniques are at the core of understanding many social phenomena. Thus, he states:

> I believe that specifically even at the depth of our mystical states there are body techniques [...] I think that there have to be biological ways of "communicating with the divine."[42]

This strand of anthropological thought that is concerned with *practice* as a *foundational* to a system of ideas is not often made explicit in the history of anthropology. Shannon, for instance, claims that there are inadequacies in the anthropological study of ritual, namely, these studies emphasise the "element of belief (faith, doctrine, ideology, meaning) while neglecting the importance of the sensate body in ritual."[43] This is a situation much present across social sciences and humanities. Andrew Hewitt, to give an example from dance, has only recently suggested that the main political significance of dance is primarily in its praxis. He explains:

> [...] dance [can serve] as the aesthetic medium that most consistently [seeks] to understand art as something immanently political: that is, as something that derives its political significance from its own status as praxis rather than from its adherence to a logically prior political ideology located elsewhere, outside art.[44]

This quotation does not, however, imply that we should abandon looking at ideologies that surround and contextualise diverse dance practices, and it is useful to point out here that Kapferer's call to observe ritual practice in its own right does *not* mean neglecting or ignoring social, political and cultural notions that surround and contextualise the performance. What I suggest here is looking, on the one hand, at a more balanced interplay between viewing ritual as socio-cultural expression and viewing it as a choreographed event. On the other hand I suggest re-reading ethnographic accounts of performance events to tease out those moments of methodological and empirical insecurities that shape performance ethnographies. Take, for instance, the now already classic

---

[42] Marcel Mauss, "Techniques of the Body," Trans. Ben Brewster, Economy and Society 2, no. 1 (1973): 386.
[43] Jonathan J. Shannon, "The aesthetics of spiritual practice and the creation of moral and musical subjectivities in Aleppo, Syria," Ethnology 43, no. 4 (2004): 382.
[44] Andrew Hewitt, *Social Choreography: Ideology as Performance in Dance and Everyday Movement* (Durham and London: Duke University Press, 2005), 6.

---

tale of the shaman Quesalid, a Kwakiutl who wanted to expose shamanic quackery. Lévi-Strauss borrowed the tale from Franz Boas' ethnography and offered a full version in his work *Structural Anthropology*. Although Lévi-Strauss emphasises the element of belief in the process of shamanic healing he undoubtedly sees the whole process as *performative* in nature. He describes it as "threefold experience" that includes "first [...] the shaman himself, who, if his calling is the true one [...] undergoes specific states of a psychosomatic nature; second, that of a sick person, who may or may not experience an improvement of his condition; and, finally, that of the public, who also participates in the cure, experiencing an enthusiasm and an intellectual and emotional satisfaction which produce collective support."[45] Richard Schechner then took and further re-examined Quesalid's story to emphasise the importance of body techniques and skills in understanding the effectiveness of magic in ritual. The story is worth quoting in length because it has found its way into several accounts of both anthropologists and performance studies scholars over several decades:

> Driven by curiosity about their tricks and by the desire to expose them, [Quesalid] began to associate with the shamans until one of them offered to make him a member of their group. Quesalid did not wait to be asked twice. He was thoroughly trained in acting, magic, singing; he learned how to fake fainting and fits, how to induce vomiting, and how to employ spies who would tell him about the lives of his patients. He learned how to hide a wad of down in the corner of his mouth and then, biting his tongue or making his gums bleed, to produce this bloody evidence before patients and spectators [...] Quesalid mastered the art so well that he not only exposed other shamans as quacks but built a powerful reputation for himself as a true shaman. Over the years he began to believe in his cures, even though he knew that they were based on tricks. He reasoned that the ill got better because they believed in him because he knew his art so well and performed it so stunningly. Finally he thought of the bloody down and all other tricks as manifestations of his own authentic powers. [...] Quesalid, like the leopard in Kafka's parable, was absorbed in the field of his own performing. He was absorbed into what he had set out to expose.[46]

Schechner quotes this story from Lévi-Strauss to comment on performing as "faking the truth" until it "becomes the truth," or "as an exemplar of the

---

[45] Claude Lévi-Strauss, Structural Anthropology (New York: Basic Books, 1963), 179.
[46] Schechner, *Between Theater*, 121.

epistemological predicaments and postmodern paradoxes of performance."[47]
Schechner emphasises how Lévi-Strauss explained Quesalid's success
purely in psychological terms, thus neglecting the aspects of performance.
Dwight Conquergood, another performance studies scholar, commented
on the same story concluding that "[w]hat is missing from Lévi-Strauss's
discussion of Quesalid is a performative appreciation for historical
process, how practices accumulatively interact and develop through time,
reconstituting agent and agency and reconfiguring context."[48] Therefore,
although the story as such emphasises the fact that Quesalid was able to
cure his patients because they *believed* that he had the powers, it is also
significant to note that Quesalid was aware that the reason also lay in the
fact that he was able to *perform* his tricks *so stunningly*.

Michael Taussig, in his writings on shamanism and healing, has been
more direct in taking on Mauss's idea of body techniques being at the core
of a shaman's work in the curing of his/her patient and also expands,
unintentionally, on some aspects of Quesalid's story. Taussig emphasises
the "motion of the tricks" or fluidity with which the shaman performs as
being of vital interest for understanding the effectiveness of the cure.
Firstly he calls this fluidity "sheer becoming in which being and nonbeing
are transformed into the beingness of transforming forms"[49] thus building
on the aspect of performance theory that is coming from the vitalist
tradition of Deleuze and Guattari. Secondly, Taussig's work on
shamanistic healing is important for Performance Studies in one other
critical instance. Namely, Taussig compares this fluidity with mimesis
suggesting mimesis as "a sort of streaming metamorphicity rather than
replication as with a photograph"[50] and it is this critical reworking of the
concept of mimesis that deserves further attention. Relying on the work of
Hokheimer and Adorno, especially of the *Dialectic of Enlightenment*
Taussig understands mimesis as "both the faculty of imitation and the
deployment of that faculty in sensuous knowing, sensuous Othering."[51]
Thus Taussig states that:

---

[47] Dwight Conquergood, "Performance Theory, Hmong Shamans, and Cultural Politics," in Critical Theory and Performance, ed. Janelle Reinelt and Joseph Roach (Ann Arbor: University of Michigan Press, 1992), 41.
[48] Ibid.
[49] Michael Taussig, Walter Benjamin's Grave (Chicago and London: University of Chicago Press, 2006), 140.
[50] Ibid.
[51] Michael Taussig, Mimesis and Alterity: A Particular History of the Senses (New York: Routledge, 1993), 68.

[t]he wonder of mimesis lies in the copy drawing on the character and power of the original, to the point whereby the representation may even assume that character and that power.[52]

Although Taussig here reworks the concept of mimesis (both a philosophical and aesthetic concept and a fundamental category of aesthetics and poetics) in developing his theory of magic healing, it carries a strong significance for Performance Studies where anti-representational movement/impulse has a strong influence. Lather, for instance, outlines this trend in performance ethnography by calling for "posthumanist materialism" that "shifts from mimesis to something altered and altering in its approach to language and history."[53] Denzin gives several ways of understanding mimesis in performance and theatre—namely, as imitation (*mimesis*); construction (*poiesis*) and as a motion of movement (*kinesis*).[54] We could easily situate Taussig's work within this continuum. Relying on Conquergood, Denzin also suggests ethnographers should move away from viewing performance as imitation, dramaturgical staging, liminality or construction in order to better view performance "[...] as struggle, as intervention, as breaking and remaking, as kinesis, as a sociopolitical act."[55] In general, this shift away from classical notions of mimesis inherent in traditional drama has been widely noted with the emergence of postdramatic theatre forms,[56] but my question is whether there is a place to discuss mimesis in performing arts *via* an anthropology of magic. Throughout theatre history (not just from Brook's vision of the "Holy Theatre,"[57]not just through the decades of avant-garde performances, not just Dolan's "utopian performative,") theatre directors, actors and scholars have explored and envisioned the "magical" nature of theatre performance. Take for example Copeau's 1923 Geneva address where he describes the "true audience" almost as ritual participants where its members "gather [and] wait together in common urgency, and their tears and laughter incorporate them almost physically into the drama or comedy that we perform."[58] However, some recent discussion on the nature of "theatre

---

[52] Ibid., xiii.
[53] Lather, "Working the Ruins," 205.
[54] Norman K. Denzin, Performance Ethnography: Critical Pedagogy and the Politics of Culture (Thousand Oaks; London; New Delhi: Sage Publications, 2003)
[55] Ibid., 4.
[56] Hans-Thies Lehmann, Postdramatic Theatre (London: Routledge, 2006).
[57] Peter Brook, The Empty Space (New York: Avon, 1969).
[58] Jacques Copeau, *Notes sur le métier de comédien* (Paris: Michel Brient, 1955), 38-9, quoted in Phillip Auslander, *From Acting to Performance: Essays in Modernism and Postmodernism* (London: Routledge, 1997), 16.

magic" suggests different avenues of understanding. Gay's McAuley's *Not Magic But Work: An Ethnographic Account of a Rehearsal Process* offers a theoretical framework for rehearsal practices in order to reject the simplistic idea of a director's individual genius as a creator of the "theatre magic." Instead, it focuses on the nature of collaborative *work* during the rehearsal process—everyday rehearsal practices including coffee drinking, birthday celebrations and costume making. My intention here, similarly to McAuley, is to deconstruct the "magic of theatre" experience by looking at anthropological accounts of magic and ritual (yet again).

In this respect I again return to ritual, most specifically Bruce Kapferer's understanding of the relation between ritual reality and the realities external to ritual. Drawing from Deleuze and Guattari, Kapferer uses the term *virtuality* to speak about the reality of ritual. At the outset, Kapferer clarifies that his idea of virtuality differs from the virtuality of cyber technologies insofar as he see the virtuality of the ritual as reality of its own— "which is neither simulacrum of external reality, nor an alternative reality."[59] As such, a ritual is neither a copy of existing reality nor an alternative (utopian) reality, but "a dynamic space entirely to itself and subject to its own emergent logics."[60] In a nutshell, Kapferer offers a fresh view on the reality of magic and ritual as follows:

> The cosmology in which its inner praxis is articulated has no necessary connection to realities external to it and no necessary internal consistency. Indeed, the imagery of what I call the phantasmatic (virtual) space of magic and sorcery (and, also, much ritual) is likely to build out of numerous sources, both personal and historical [...] What I stress is that the potency of much magical practice is in this virtuality—which stands outside of all reason—even, perhaps, its own. As such it contains its own "truth" [...].[61]

But what is the role of this inner truth of magic/ritual? Kapferer follows Deleuze and Guattari to conclude that the external reality, the lived-in-life that he terms *actuality* is a chaotic and indeterminate space and the role of the ritual is to enter "within life's vital processes and [adjust] its dynamic."[62] Henceforth,

---

[59] Kapferer, *The Fest of the Sorcerer*, 37.
[60] Ibid., 7.
[61] Kapferer, "Outside All Reason," 23.
[62] Ibid., 48.

[t]he apparent repetitive dynamic of so much ritual is a dimension of the radical slowing down in the virtuality of the rite of the tempo of ordinary life, its speed, continuous shifts in standpoint, changes in perspective and structures of context—the chaos of lived experience.[63]

Note here how Kapferer's vision of the ritual reality differs from Turner's notion of limen. To Turner it is precisely the limen that is the chaotic, indeterminate space which subsequently affirms or subverts the external reality. In any case, the limen is either mirror or inverted mirror of external reality. We can see that to Kapferer there is no straightforward and assumed connection between these realities—and the external reality (*actuality*) is the one that is chaotic and indeterminate. The other important aspect of Kapferer's work on ritual is the issue of repetition and it is useful here to distinguish and clarify two modes of repetition which are conceptually related although they operate differently. The broader mode of ritual repetition is connected to the periodic repetition of the entire performance including the existing gaps between the repetitions, it includes the temporal dimension.[64] The other mode is a repetition that occurs "within a single ritual, and is experienced as a steady, unbroken flow [...]."[65] The broader mode of repetition, repetition *of* the ritual is what usually concerns anthropologists when they write about rituals to explain their social and cultural effectiveness. However, Kapferer pays equal attention to the repetition *in* ritual. Kapferer's term repetition in ritual

[...] has importance for much more that being definitional of rite or functional for the communication of its message or meaning [...] [W]hat is seen as repetition, the apparent obsession with detail, precision, and so forth, is an expression of the constitutive and generative aspects of practice: that is, practice not as a representation of meanings but the very dynamic of their constitution.[66]

Finally, Kapferer considers the body and organisation of sense and sensuous experience in ritual. In reworking an older body vs culture debate Kapferer claims that:

---

[63] Ibid.
[64] Margaret Drewal, Yoruba Ritual: performance, play, agency (Bloomington: Indiana University Press, 1992), 2.
[65] Ibid.
[66] Kapferer, *The Fest of the Sorcerer*, 178.

[…] the force of much ritual may be in the dynamics of the rite qua dynamics, in the way sensory perception is dynamically organized, which then simultaneously becomes the ground and the force behind the meaningful constructions that are woven into the dynamics.[67]

So it is neither body nor culture that gives the ritual its meaning, but the dynamics between them in the moment of performance, in the virtuality of the ritual. I am suggesting the observation of performance events as the kind of virtual reality implied in Kapferer's study of ritual. The issues of repetition, precision, body techniques and even mimetic representation are at the core of anthropological concerns with magic and ritual but they can also shed some light onto the "magic of the theatre" experience.

Conclusion

In more general ways, however, the connecting tissue between anthropology and performance studies in the twenty-first century will be the issue of ethnography and ethnographic writing. Ethnographic fieldwork research and writings connects beyond anthropology and performance studies and is being recognised, for instance, "as the absolute *sine qua non* of the folklore profession."[68] The notion of fieldwork research has been explored, theorised and developed within anthropology. Clifford Geertz once said that "[d]oing ethnography is like trying to read […] a manuscript,"[69] but those days seem long gone. Fabian, for instance, called for a turn "from informative to performative ethnography […] an ethnography of the ears and heart that reimagines participant-observation as performative witnessing."[70] Similarly Pink called for "sensory ethnography"[71] and Englund coined the term "emplacement"[72] to account

---

[67] Kapferer, "Ritual Dynamics and Virtual Practice," 41.

[68] Steven J. Zeitlin, "I'm a Folklorist and You're Not: Expansive versus Delimited Strategies in the Practice of Folklore," The Journal of American Folklore 113, no. 447 (2000): 3-19.

[69] Clifford Geertz, *Interpretations of Cultures* (New York: Basic Books, 1973), 10, quoted in Dwight Conquergood, "Performance Studies: Interventions and Radical Research," The Drama Review 46, no. 2 (2002): 150.

[70] Johannes Fabian, *Power and Performance: Ethnographic Explorations Through Proverbial Wisdom and Theater* in Shaba, Zaire (Madison: University of Wisconsin Press, 1990), 3, quoted in Dwight Conquergood, "Performance Studies: Interventions and Radical Research," The Drama Review 46, no. 2 (2002): 149.

[71] Sarah Pink, Doing Sensory Ethnography (London: Sage Publications, 2009).

[72] Harri Englund, "Ethnography after Globalism: Migration and emplacement in Malawi," American Ethnologist 29, no. 2 (2002): 261-286.

for the experience of writing ethnography in globalisation. The latest issue of *Canadian Theatre Review* is entirely dedicated to a reconnection of early work in the ethnography of performance with contemporary practices of performance ethnography. The issue gathered work across the disciplines of folklore, anthropology, communication and ethnomusicology to employ ethnographic methods to debate practice-as-research in performing arts and critical pedagogy. The issue in question "demonstrates the transformative vitality of ethnographic practices in the analysis, analyzing, devising, and pedagogy of performance."[73]

Turning to the "transformative vitality of ethnographic practices" is a good way to end this chapter. I hope that I have managed to outline some of the parameters for a future collaboration between anthropology and performance studies.

Works Cited

Alexander, Jeffrey C. "Cultural Pragmatics: Social Performance between ritual and strategy." *Sociological Theory* 22, no. 4 (2004): 527-573.

Barba, Eugenio. "Theatre Anthropology." *The Drama Review* 94, no. 2 (1982): 5-32.

Bauman, Richard. *Verbal Art as Performance*, vii. Rowley Mass., 1977. Quoted in Simon J. Bronner, "Art, Performance, and Praxis: The Rhetoric of Contemporary Folklore Studies." Western Folklore 47, no. 2 (1988): 87.

Beeman, William O. "The Anthropology of Theater and Spectacle." *Annual Review of Anthropology* 22 (1993): 369-393.

Brook, Peter. *The Empty Space*. New York: Avon, 1969.

Buckland, Theresa. "All Dances are Ethnic, but Some Are More Ethnic Than Others: Some Observations on Dance Studies and Anthropology." *Dance Research: The Journal for the Society of Dance Research* 17, no. 1 (1999): 3-21.

Clifford, James, and George Marcus. *Writing Culture: the Poetics and Politics of Ethnography*. Los Angeles and London: University of California Press, 1986.

Conquergood, Dwight. "Performance Theory, Hmong Shamans, and Cultural Politics" In *Critical Theory and Performance*, edited by

---

[73] Rusted, "Editor's note."

Janelle Reinelt and Joseph Roach, 41-65. Ann Arbor: The University of Michigan Press, 1992.

—. "Performance Studies: Interventions and Radical Research." *The Drama Review* 46, no. 2 (2002): 145-156.

Copeau, Jacques. *Notes sur le métier de comédien*, 38-39. Paris: Michel Brient, 1955. Quoted in Phillip Auslander, *From Acting to Performance: Essays in Modernism and Postmodernism* (London: Routledge, 1997), 16.

Denzin, Norman K. *Performance Ethnography: Critical Pedagogy and the Politics of Culture*. Thousand Oaks; London; New Delhi: Sage Publications: 2003.

Desmond, Jane. "Terra Incognita: Mapping New Territory in Dance and 'Cultural Studies'" *Dance Research Journal* 32, no. 1 (2000): 43-53.

Dolan, Jill. "Producing Knowledges That Matter: Practicing Performance Studies through Theatre Studies." *The Drama Review* 40, no. 4 (1996): 9-19.

—. "Performance, Utopia, and 'Utopian Performative'" *Theatre Journal* 53, no. 3 (2001): 455-479.

Drewal, Margaret. *Yoruba Ritual: performers, play, agency*. Bloomington: Indiana University Press, 1992.

Englund, Harri. "Ethnography after Globalism: Migration and Emplacement in Malawi." *American Ethnologist* 29, no. 2 (2002): 261-286.

Fabian, Johannes. *Power and Performance: Ethnographic Explorations Through Proverbial Wisdom and Theater in Shaba, Zaire*, 3. Madison: University of Wisconsin Press, 1990. Quoted in Dwight Conquergood, "Performance Studies: Interventions and Radical Research." The Drama Review 46, no. 2 (2002): 149.

Farnell, Brenda. "Ethno-Graphic and the moving body." *Man, New Series* 29 (1994): 929-974.

Foster, Susan L. *Choreographing Empathy: Kinesthesia in Performance*. London: Routledge, 2011.

Geertz, Clifford. *The Interpretations of Cultures*, 10. New York: Basic Books, 1973. Quoted in Dwight Conquergood, "Performance Studies: Interventions and Radical Research." The Drama Review 46, no. 2 (2002): 150.

Geertz, Clifford. "Blurred Genres." *American Scholar* 49, no. 2 (1980):165-182.

Handelman, Don. "Why Ritual in Its Own Right?" In *Ritual in its own right: Exploring the Dynamics of Transformation*, edited by Don Handelman and Galina Lindquist, 1-35. New York: Berghahn Books, 2004.

Hewitt, Andrew. *Social Choreography: Ideology as Performance in Dance and Everyday Movement*. Durham and London: Duke University Press, 2005.

Kapchan, Deborah. "Performance." *The Journal of American Folklore* 108, no. 430 (1995): 479-508.

Kapferer, Bruce. *The Feast of the Sorcerer: Practices of Consciousness and Power*. Chicago: The University of Chicago Press, 1997.

—. "Introduction: Outside All Reason: Magic, Sorcery, and Epistemology in Anthropology." In *Beyond Rationalism: Rethinking Magic, Witchcraft and Sorcery*, edited by Bruce Kapferer, 1-31. New York: Berghahn Books, 2002.

—. "Ritual Dynamics and Virtual Practice: Beyond Representation and Meaning." In *Ritual in its own right: Exploring the Dynamics of Transformation*, edited by Don Handelman and Galina Lindquist, 35-55. New York: Berghahn Books, 2004.

Lather, Patti. "Working the Ruins of Feminist Ethnography." *Signs* 27, no. 1 (2001): 199-227.

Lehmann, Hans-Thies. *Postdramatic Theatre*. London: Routledge, 2006.

Lévi-Strauss, Claude. *Structural Anthropology*. Trans. Claire Jacobson and Brooke Grundfest. New York: Basic Books, 1963.

Mauss, Marcel. "Techniques of the Body." Trans. Ben Brewster. *Economy and Society* 2, no. 1 (1973): 70-88.

McAuley, Gay. *Not Magic But Work: An Ethnographic Account of a Rehearsal Process*. Manchester: Manchester University Press, 2012.

McKenzie, Jon. *Perform or Else: From Discipline to Performance*. New York: Routledge, 2001.

—. "Democracy's Performance." *The Drama Review* 47, no. 2 (2003): 117-128.

Mock, Roberta, and Ruth Way. "Pedagogies of Theatre (Arts) and Performance (Studies)." *Studies in Theatre and Performance* 25, no. 3 (2005): 201-213.

Pink, Sarah. *Doing Sensory Ethnography*. London: Sage Publications, 2009.

Rusted, Brian. "Editor's note." *Canadian Theatre Review* 151, (2012).

Schechner, Richard. *Between Theater and Anthropology*. Philadelphia: University of Pennsylvania Press, 1985.

—. *The Future of Ritual: Writings on culture and performance*. London and New York: Routledge, 1995.

Shannon, Jonathan J. "The aesthetics of spiritual practice and the creation of moral and musical subjectivities in Aleppo, Syria." *Ethnology* 43, no. 4 (2004): 381-391.

Sklar, Deidre. "On Dance Ethnography." *Dance Research Journal* 32, no. 1 (2000): 70-77.

St John, Graham. "An Introduction." In *Victor Turner and Contemporary Cultural Performance,* edited by Graham St John, 1-38. New York: Berghahn Book, 2008.

Taussig, Michael. *Mimesis and Alterity: A Particular History of the Senses.* New York: Routledge, 1993.

—. *Walter Benjamin's Grave.* Chicago and London: Chicago University Press, 2006.

Turner, Victor. *The Forest of Symbols: Aspects of Ndembu Ritual.* New York; London: Cornell University Press, 1970.

—. *From Ritual to Theatre: the human seriousness of play.* New York: PAJ Publications, 1982.

Watson, Ian. *Negotiating Cultures: Eugenio Barba and the Intercultural Debate.* Manchester: Manchester University Press, 2002.

Werbner, Pnina, and Helene Basu. "The Embodiment of Charisma." In *Embodying Charisma: Modernity, Locality, and the Performance of Emotion in Sufi Cults,* edited by Pnina Werbner and Helene Basu, 3-29. London: Routledge, 1998.

Zeitlin, Steven J. "I'm a Folklorist and You're Not: Expansive versus Delimited Strategies in the Practice of Folklore." *The Journal of American Folklore* 113, no. 447 (2000): 3-19.

CHAPTER THREE

WAYS OF MOVING AND THINKING: THE EMPLACED BODY AS A TOOL FOR ETHNOGRAPHIC RESEARCH

ANN DAVID

This chapter attempts to take a fresh look at the utilisation of embodied ethnography, focusing on the centrality of bodily experience as a key tool for understanding dance practice and dance knowledge. I explore how the emplaced body and lived experience (of the researcher) can yield deeper levels of understanding and insight through engaged practice on different levels of immersion, using several detailed examples from my own fieldwork researching a variety of dance genres. The discussion is set in the context of the relatively new interest in the body in various academic disciplines including sociology, anthropology, religious studies, and philosophy, where lived practice through the ethnographer's and participants' bodies may be privileged. It also maps the older and more substantially articulated debates relating to embodied knowledge common in the disciplines of dance studies and ethnomusicology. Academics working in dance studies with an ethnographic or anthropological focus, for example, Theresa Buckland's research on the Coconut Britannia dancers of the UK,[1] Andrée Grau's fieldwork with Aboriginal Tiwi groups in Northern Australia,[2] Tomie Hahn and her embodied research on the Japanese *nihon buyo*,[3] Felicia Hughes-Freeland and her work with Javanese

---

[1] Theresa Buckland, ed., Dance in the Field: Theory, Methods and Issues in Dance Ethnography (Basingstoke: Macmillan, 1999); and Buckland Theresa, ed., Dancing From Past to Present: Nation, Culture, Identities (Wisconsin: University of Wisconsin Press, 2006).

[2] Andreé Grau, "Tiwi Dance Aesthetics," Yearbook for Traditional Music 35, (2003): 175-180.

[3] Tomie Hahn, Sensational Knowledge: Embodying Culture through Japanese Dance (Middletown, Conn: Wesleyan University Press, 2007).

dance,[4] as well as Sally Ann Ness[5] and Deidre Sklar[6] focus on the understanding of layered knowledge through the dance experience of the researcher and researched.

In a similar way, other non-dance writers using a variety of theoretical frameworks and emerging from different academic backgrounds feature ethnographic embodiment in their work. I am thinking here of the published writing of scholars such as Kirsty Nabhan-Warren[7] and Thomas Tweed[8] in religious studies, who note the essential embodiedness that forms the core of religious practice; Sarah Pink[9] in sensory ethnography, and Helen Thomas and Jamila Ahmed[10] in sociology as examples of this. Working and dancing with people not only brings a deep involvement and personal engagement, but has the power to transcend issues of representation, class distinction, hetero-normative boundaries and post-colonial differences that abound in the ethnographic fieldwork setting. Practitioner and performance studies academic Jerri Daboo writing her ethnography on neo-Tarentism in contemporary Salento, southern Italy, reveals "how body and performance can be seen as the embodiment of past and present and how the process of engagement with the act of performance creates a sense of presence in the specific spatial-temporal location."[11] My own dance fieldwork that examines dance and the social, cultural, economic and political factors framing such practices, ranges

---

[4] Felicia Hughes-Freeland, "Dance on Film: Strategy and Serendipity," in Dance in the Field: Theory, Methods and Issues in Dance Ethnography, ed. Theresa Buckland, 111-122 (Basingstoke: Macmillan, 1999).
[5] Sally Ann Ness, Body, Movement, and Culture: Kinesthetic and Visual Symbolism in a Philippine Community (Philadelphia: University of Pennsylvania Press, 1992).
[6] Deidre Sklar, Dancing with the Virgin: Body and Faith in the Fiesta of Tortugas, New Mexico (Berkeley, California: University of California Press, 2001).
[7] Kirsty Nabhan-Warren, "Embodied Research and Writing: A Case for Phenomenologically Oriented Religious Studies Ethnographies," Journal of the American Academy of Religion 79, no. 2 (2011): 378-407.
[8] Thomas Tweed, Crossing and Dwelling: A Theory of Religion (Boston: Harvard University Press, 2006).
[9] Sarah Pink, Doing Sensory Ethnography (London: Sage Publications, 2009).
[10] Helen Thomas and Jamila Ahmed, eds., Cultural Bodies: Ethnography and Theory (Oxford: Blackwell Publishing, 2004).
[11] Jerri Daboo, Ritual, Rupture, and Remorse: A Study of Tarantism and Pizzica in Salento (Oxford: Peter Lang, 2010), 39.

from Polish traditional dancers to Hindu folk and classical dance, and religious danced rituals, and will serve to illustrate the arguments made.[12]

The theme of the conference[13] out of which this collection of chapters arises already considers the problematics of terminology. It questions what is meant by "contemporary ethnography" and "traditional" performance (the call for papers even states "whatever that might mean"). Are we referring to the significant debates that range around issues of alternative ethnographic methods such as analytic or evocative autoethnographies?[14] Or engaging with expressions such as realist ethnography, or performed ethnography, or even simply postmodern ethnography? Scholars are well aware of how the term "traditional" is often now considered a rather inadequate word in performance terms, used dismissively to imply fixity and lack of innovation or an unquestioned narrative linking contemporary practices with a mythic past that has no objective reality. Yet of course, as dance academic and practitioner Janet O'Shea notes, "Concepts of authenticity, tradition, classicism, and history do not necessarily invoke agreement; rather, they form the basis of diverse points of view."[15] So, here we have several issues for debate and I will try to touch on these as I move through this chapter.

---

[12] See Ann R. David, "Local Diasporas/Global Trajectories: New Aspects of Religious 'Performance' in British Tamil Hindu Practice," Performance Research 13, no. 3 (2008): 89-99; Ann R. David, "Performing for the Gods? Dance and Embodied Ritual in British Hindu Temples," South Asian Popular Culture 7, no. 3 (2009): 217-231; Ann R. David, "Gendering the Divine: New Forms of Feminine Hindu Worship," International Journal of Hindu Studies 13, no. 3 (2010): 337-355; Ann R. David, "Sacralising the City: Sound, Space and Performance in Hindu Ritual Practices in London," Special Issue: Culture and Religion 13, no. 4 (2012): 449-467; Ann R. David, "Embodied traditions: Gujarati (dance) Practices of *garba* and *raas* in the UK Context," in Politics of Embodiment: Dance and Identities in a Globalized World, eds. Ann R. David and Linda Dankworth (Basingstoke, Hants: Palgrave Macmillan, 2013): forthcoming.

[13] The conference was titled "Contemporary Ethnography and Traditional Performance," and it was held at the University of Chester, UK, in July 2012.

[14] Due to constrains of space, I will not go into this area in this chapter, but much has been written on this move away from "traditional" ethnographic work. See the special issue of the Journal of Contemporary Ethnography 35, no. 4 (2006) for several articles on autoethnography.

[15] Janet O'Shea, "Dancing Through History and Ethnography: Indian Classical Dance and the Performance of the Past," in Dancing From Past to Present: Nation, Culture, Identities, ed. Theresa Buckland (Wisconsin: University of Wisconsin Press, 2006), 125.

My own background is not in performance studies, as it is known in the USA and in the UK, although I am well aware of the importance of bodily engagement and its theoretical paradigms within the discipline of Performance Studies. An education in dance (ballet, contemporary, folk and Indian classical) and a particular and long-lasting interest in the social, political and cultural ideas in and around the various forms of dance, led me to a training in anthropological and ethnographical approaches to human movement. The questions of who dances (as well as who does not dance), the where and how, as well as the when and the why lead one into a detailed exploration of dance and movement genres that can reveal a multivalent, highly nuanced understanding of how dancers, and non-dancers think, feel, know and act out their lives. So I am here focusing on the very acts of ethnographic fieldwork and will explore some of the advantages and difficulties of embodying and experiencing that fieldwork as a researcher and a dancer. I look at the varying degrees of participation and seek to find what sort of understanding might be gained in this way. And of course, we need to remember how both anthropology and sociology have been extremely significant in the development of the approach of performance studies that itself embraces fully the notion of the centrality and presence of bodily knowledge.[16]

In the development of the anthropology of dance, the understanding as Grau puts it, of "'Bodily intelligence' and 'performative modes of thought'"[17] has been a central issue. Hughes-Freeland, who used her own body's learning to understand the intricacies of Javanese dance and its systems of mnemonics for choreography, describes how for her, dancing is a "physical dimension of human existence which is at once embodied and imagined, and I have researched dancing to examine how social values, real and ideal, are embodied."[18] Hahn discusses what she calls enactive knowledge, when her Japanese dance teacher during a *nihon buyo* lesson told her to "Know with your body."[19] In this instance, it involved a complex embodying of the Japanese concept of flow of energy around and through the body, and a sensitivity to it that could not be necessarily seen

[16] See Daboo, op.cit. Norman K. Denzin, Performance Ethnography: Critical Pedagogy and the Politics of Culture (Thousand Oaks; London; New Delhi: Sage Publications, 2003).
[17] Andrée Grau, "Fieldwork, Politics and Power," in Dance in the Field: Theory, Methods and Issues in Dance Ethnography, ed. Theresa Buckland (Basingstoke: Macmillan, 1999), 166.
[18] Hughes-Freeland, 113.
[19] Hahn, 1.

from the outside. Buckland in stressing how "Embodied practice…
underlines the power of the performative"[20] notes how the recent interest
in the body and bodily performance in disciplines outside of dance
anthropology in the humanities and social sciences has not only "helped
raise the profile of dance as a significant academic site for cultural
investigation"[21] but has also opened up the dialogue on the body with
these other scholarly areas.

As far as the discipline of ethnomusicology is concerned, the long
tradition has been to participate in musical performance in the field, as
anthropologist and musicologist Tina K. Ramnarine points out, "In terms
of pedagogic as well as research strategies, performance as learning has
long been a central issue to ethnomusicologists."[22] Gaining a fluency in
non-western musical forms not only provides an experiential approach, but
also gives a way of understanding "different societies and systems of
thought."[23] American ethnomusicologist Mantle Hood theorised this fluency
in two or more musical systems as "bi-musicality,"[24] taking the term from
the linguistic notion of bilingual. The idea draws strongly from certain
anthropological approaches that through participation, a deeper
understanding of the people being studied may be gained, and not just
their musical forms. As Jeff Todd Titon, ethnomusicologist, wrote "Bi-
musicality…can induce moments of what I call *culture shift*, when one
acquires knowledge by figuratively stepping outside oneself to view the
world with oneself in it, thereby becoming both subject and object
simultaneously. Bi-musicality in this way becomes a figure for a path
toward understanding."[25] The development of the famous ethnomusicology
programmes at Queen's University, Belfast was largely due to the early
work of Hood (at UCLA, USA) and by ethnomusicologist John Blacking,

---

[20] Buckland, "Dance Authenticity," 13.

[21] Ibid., 1.

[22] Tina K. Ranmarine, "Performance and Experimental Learning in the Study of
Ethnomusicology," in Learning Fields: Current Policies and Practices in European
Social Anthropology Education, eds. Dorie Drackle and Iain Edgar (Oxford and
New York: Berghahn Books, 2004), 227.

[23] Ibid., 228.

[24] Mantle Hood, "The Challenge of 'Bi-musicality,'" Ethnomusicology 4, no. 2
(1960): 55-59.

[25] Jeff Todd Titon, "Bi-Musicality as Metaphor," The Journal of American
Folklore 108, no. 429 (1995): 228. Emphasis original; see also Andrée Grau,
"Dance, Anthropology, and Research through Practice" (paper presented at the
CORD conference, Paris, France, 2007), 1-7.

appointed Chair of Social Anthropology in Belfast in 1970. Blacking saw
the participation in the field and the analysis of the data gathered as parts
of one whole; as Grau, one of his students there wrote, "so that two kinds
of technical knowledge and experience are confronted, and informants can
share in the intellectual process of analysis."[26] Blacking's approach was
that learning to play and to perform music was a basic field technique of
ethnomusicology; through his work, ethnomusicology and dance
anthropology became established as a subject area of special interest at
Queen's.

Ethnomusicology's insistence on participation through performing, is I
believe, of value to all dance ethnographers, in that it may help to
surmount the problems of getting "under the skin" in our fieldwork
situations. Social anthropologist Clifford Geertz writes of the difficulty for
ethnographers in "getting themselves into the culture"[27] and his work and
writings (despite the twenty-year gap) are relevant here. Some of the
considerations that have arisen when I once more found myself at *that*
stage in the ethnographic process—the stage where we find ourselves
questioning the very nature of our fieldwork, interrogating our very
presence in the field, and probing the many ethical issues and intricate
politics emerging—and I began to reflect again on the meaning of Geertz's
well-known phrases of "Being There" and "Being Here."[28] The oscillation
of the ethnographer from field site to home and back again is a process
more complex than is often considered in the first stages of ethnographic
enquiry, and one that in fact requires constant revisiting through
questioning and self-reflexive looking.[29] In terms of participant work,
what does "being here" and "being there" actually mean? Geertz questions

---

[26] Andrée Grau, "John Blacking and the Development of Dance anthropology in
the United Kingdom," Dance Research Journal 25, no. 2 (1993): 25.
[27] Clifford Geertz, Works and Lives: The Anthropologist as Author (Stanford,
California: Stanford University Press, 1988), 17.
[28] Ibid., 1 and 129.
[29] I am aware of the debates raised in anthropology about the notion of the
"ethnographic present" where discussion about the double-sidedness of fieldwork
practice (home and away; observation and analysis) is current (see in particular:
Narmala Halstead and others, eds., *Knowing How to Know: Fieldwork and the
Ethnographic Present* [New York and Oxford: Berghahn Books, 2008]). "New
moments of knowing" are seen as part of long-term and continuous engagement in
the field, and the "ethnographic present as shaped by changing historical consciousness
and embedded in processes of history" (Narmala Halstead, "Introduction:
Experiencing the Ethnographic Present: Knowing through 'Crisis,'" eds. Narmala
Halstead and others [New York and Oxford: Berghahn Books], 7).

how do you "speak not just *about* another form of life but ... speak from within it"—a process he terms "ethnographic ventriloquism."[30] How does one allow the practices, the understanding, and the subsequent text when it is written to be polyvalent and polysemic, giving presence and power to all those on whom it is dependant? How does one "gain a working familiarity with the frames of meaning"[31] within which ones' fellow contributors conduct their lives? These questions that deal with the inhabiting of ethnography's double fields—the field-site and back home, as anthropologist Marilyn Strathern put it,[32] and the debate regarding the importance of the ethnographic present, or moment, when those two fields merge, if briefly, in a moment of understanding[33] are some of the most significant queries facing most anthropologists engaging with ethnography.

In attempting to answer some of these questions, my emphasis will be the focus on the body—the use of the lived body to understand both ourselves and the lifeworlds of our contributors and our participants. Watching, observing in detail, but even more importantly, participating in the movement and dance clearly allows a deeper level of engagement, and looks to the body as a source of knowledge. As dance ethnologist Deidre Sklar states, "the way people move provides a key to the way that they think and feel and to what they know."[34] This approach focuses on the people and their movement systems as expressions of cultural knowledge rather than the society as a whole. Not only the obvious forms of dance and movement systems, but all actions, rhythms, postures, ways of doing can express what is hidden behind the obvious physical manifestation. Hence an exploration of such practices reveals the concealed cultural codes, and displays the conceptual thought and words that bind a community and in which their history, traditions, beliefs, knowledges, and communications are held. In this way the invisible culture of a society is made visible through its representations in its dance and movement

---

[30] Ibid., 145.
[31] Clifford Geertz, Available Light: Anthropological Reflections on Philosophic Topic (Princeton and Oxford: Princeton University Press, 2000), 16.
[32] Marilyn Strathern, Property, Substance and Effect: Anthropological Essays on Persons and Things (London: Athlone Press, 1999), 2.
[33] Halstead, "Introduction," 1; Ibid., 6.
[34] Deidre Sklar, "On Dance Ethnography," Dance Research Journal 23, (1991): 6.

systems. To quote again from Sklar, "My learning", she writes, "I knew, would begin with my body."[35]

This approach is suggested here not as a way to reify the body (as has been so previously with the mind and mental cognition in terms of gathering knowledge), but to attempt to rebalance and readdress the particular notion of the levels of understanding made available through engaged work with our own bodies and with the bodies of practitioners. Brenda Farnell warns against being naïve about our ability to understand other cultures simply though our own experiences as a dancer, emphasising, "why careful observation and personal experience of dancing/moving are necessary, but not sufficient, for understanding human movement practices from an anthropological perspective."[36] She argues that we must also give "analytic attention to spoken discourse" and that to understand "talk from the body"[37] researchers need more than observation and experience of movement. To gain a deeper and more complete level of understanding, the ethnographer needs a cultural competence that comes from a variety of approaches—embodied practice, language skill and analysis, contextual knowledge and close engagement with the detailed particularities of the specific cultural practices under scrutiny.

Before we move to several of my own ethnographic fieldwork examples to examine how embodied experience can unfold these additional layers of understanding and help us to come closer to the experience of "being there" in our contributors' frames of meaning (as Geertz has stated), I will briefly refer to social anthropologist Peter Collins' consideration of the ethnographic self as a resource, the subject of his recent edited book.[38] In chapter 7 on dancing Tango, anthropologist Jonathan Skinner argues that the self is one of the key resources in ethnography, and "nowhere more so than in the anthropology of dance where it is vital that the writer dances and shares the experience of the dance, joins in with the dancers and embodies the dance"[39] Skinner sees movement as a site of cognition,

---

[35] Sklar, *Dancing with the Virgin*, 4.
[36] Brenda Farnell, "It Goes Without Saying—But Not Always," in Dance in the Field: Theory, Methods and Issues in Dance Ethnography, ed. Theresa Buckland (Basingstoke: Macmillan, 1999), 147.
[37] Ibid., 156.
[38] Peter Collins, ed., Ethnographic Self as Resource: Writing Memory and Experience into Ethnography (Oxford and New York: Berghahn Books, 2010).
[39] Jonathan Skinner, "Leading Questions and Body Memories: a Case of Phenomenology and Physical Ethnography in the Dance Interview," in

describing in detail how both thinking and learning take place through embodied movement. Recent interest and scientific experiment[40] in the concept of bodily entrainment show that the capacity for coordinated rhythmic movement achieved through pulse-based music and dance is present in human life from infancy. This facility for behavioral synchrony in movement with others can give rise to a powerful uniting force that historian William McNeill[41] calls "muscular bonding"—sense of community, cooperation and togetherness—through bodily entrainment. McNeill notes how moving together in time is pleasurable, making monotonous work easier. All these approaches emphasise the power of human embodied movement, culturally, historically and socially.

The four specific ethnographic fieldwork examples I will draw upon each illustrate different aspects of embodied practice discussed above. Each one also indicates the delicacy (and tension) of the ethnographer's position, often balanced between participation and observation. As all ethnographers acknowledge, this is a constantly shifting scenario, moving along the spectrum from full immersion in the fieldwork setting to minimal or no participation at all. The first illustration I select is a movement form where it appears it is the easiest to join in the movement. It is the Indian folk (dance) form of *garba*, prevalent at Gujarati cultural and religious events worldwide, and in the UK where I have carried out my fieldwork. *Garba* is traditionally played only by women (and here I am deliberately not using the word dance)[42] although now both here and in India, men will join in. The dance forms described are part of a nine-day Hindu religious festival, *Navratri* (literally nine days) that falls in the autumn and that celebrates the female aspect of the divine, *Devi*. Participants (of all ages) move in anti-clockwise concentric circles around a central shrine, known as a *garbo,* with a simple 3-clap, 4-step rhythm. At

---

Ethnographic Self as Resource: Writing Memory and Experience into Ethnography, ed. Peter Collins (Oxford and New York: Berghahn Books, 2010), 111.

[40] For example William H. McNeill, Keeping Together in Time: Dance and Drill in Human History (Cambridge MA: Cambridge University Press, 1995); and Jessica Phillips-Silver and others, "The Ecology of Entrainment: Foundations of Coordinated Rhythmic Movement," Music Perception: An Interdisciplinary Journal 28, no. 1 (2010): 3-14.

[41] McNeill, 2.

[42] These movement practices are never termed "dance" by the Gujarati community, as the word does not relate to movement practices embedded within a religious tradition. One "plays" garba (*garba ramavo*).

the midpoint of the evening, the movement will stop, and all gather round the shrine for prayers and to sing devotional hymns. Observing the *garba* it is evident that it is a very informal movement of hands, feet and body that constantly repeats to the live music. This music starts slowly at the outset and the movements are walked, but as the tempi increases, the women's steps move in a more flowing manner, getting faster as the evening wears on. The handclaps are executed on the first three beats; clapping towards the left and down for the first two, and then to the right and higher for the third. Gradually more variants creep in and as the music picks up speed, the basic foot pattern may change to a step-ball-change on each foot, travelling and turning in rhythmic and patterned formations, with two claps in the sequence. Some groups even move as one whole, first several feet to the right, then back to the left, before turning again to continue anti-clockwise in a progression around the hall. The three-clap and the alternative two-clap forms of *garba* are called in Gujarati, *Be talin no garbo; ane trana no garbo.*[43]

What is not revealed by simple observation only is the effect of these repetitive movements on the body, on one's own somatic perceptions and I would suggest, the emotional centre. By playing *garba* with the women, one begins to understand how the repetitive, circular steps create an inward focus, almost blocking out external perceptions, and creating a condition of devotional energy. The movements are deep in the women's physical forms, a striking physical display of their embodiment since childhood, when they would have imbibed the repetitive folk steps and bodily inflections through a process of natural enculturation. As Buckland notes, "It can be argued that dance has a particular propensity to foreground cultural memory as embodied practice by virtue of its predominantly somatic modes of transmission."[44] When the *garba* movements stop for prayers, everyone is visibly concentrated and one might say, "prepared," for the intensity of the religious practice that follows. Some even go into trance. This condition is heightened by the music that has, as I noted earlier, increased in speed and tempi. When I have participated, as a trained dancer it is simple to copy the physical steps, and to follow the improvised and more elaborate forms as they appear, but the interior quality is of a different order. Experiencing and embodying the movement brings an inner understanding through multi-

---

[43] See David, "Embodied traditions."
[44] Theresa Buckland, "Dance, Authenticity and Cultural Memory: the Politics of Embodiment," Yearbook for Traditional Music 33, (2001): 1.

layered perceptions of the touch of the claps, the balance of the body, the pressure of the feet at each step, the energy needed at different points of the movement, the way the weight is transferred from each foot, the rhythm of the whole sequences, as well as the shape of the effort and the direction of the body. And these are certainly factors that are inaccessible simply through observation. Ethnomusicologist John Blacking[45] famously acknowledged how movements that are rhythmic and repetitive have an effect on our cognition, thereby emphasising my earlier argument relating to entrainment and "muscular bonding."

I move now, as the second illustration, to a particular Hindu ritual performance in east London, in a form of neo-Hindu worship that I have written on previously in a different context.[46] This is a new "temple," set up in an old corner shop a few years ago in a suburban area off the main high street in East Ham, and is run by a young Tamil woman from Sri Lanka. It is an unusual place, a small, local site of religious practice, where groups of predominantly Sri Lankan women (many who have been refugees) gather to participate in the rituals of Hindu worship. It is a space which appears to challenge normative Hindu practice, offering the women a place where they can embody and perform the divine, and giving them access to a religious agency that is commonly taboo in the more orthodox Brahminical Hindu worship. At this small centre, the worship is to *Amma* (Mother) as *Sakthi* (divine female power), also known as *Adhiparasakthi*, and her appearance is threefold: through the statues of *Sakthi* in the temple; through the intermediary of a male figure, referred to as Guruji, or sometimes as God; and through his words. The male *guru* lives in India and is worshipped here in East Ham through photos and statues. In my visits to the temple, I am pressed regularly to participate in the ritual, whether I would wish to or not. Not only is this unusual as a non-Hindu, but it is a privileged and auspicious position, much sought after by the devotees present. Is this an example of intensive "being there" (to return to Geertz's phrase) with this sort of engagement, and does it sit uneasily in the field? I am reminded of anthropologist Vered Amit's words, "Ethnographic fieldwork must be experienced as performed rather than just communicated in dialogue."[47] Yet one has of course to be aware of the complexity of this particular field site, questioning, as anthropologist

---

[45] John Blacking, How Musical is Man? (Seattle and London: University of Washington Press, 1973).
[46] David, "Gendering the Divine."
[47] Vered Amit, ed., Constructing the Field: Ethnographic Fieldwork in Contemporary World (London: Routledge, 2000), 1.

Johannes Fabian has done, whether this could create a situation where we are seen as "old colonizers in a new guise?"[48] For me, engaging in dance practices in the field has often appeared a more straightforward participation than in such intimate, devotional, religious ritual. Nabhan-Warren writes of her fieldwork with Mexican American Catholics in Arizona and the effects of her participation in the Mass and in carrying the statue of the Santo Nino that allowed her "a privileged glimpse into their intense Catholic devotions."[49] Similarly, engaging with ritual practices at the Hindu temple conveys a deep sense of practical devotion and of the intimate gestures performed to their Guruji. As one is pressed to join the particular part of the performance of the ritual, kneeling, chanting and rhythmically offering flower petals to the photos of their guru, the scents, the warmth, the soft touch of the petals, the colours and the repetitive invocations all add to the potential influence of the encounter. Some sense of the concentrated power and intensity of the event is definitely transmitted during such times, power that all the devotees speak of when interviewed. I am reminded here of Sklar's notion of the "somatic, or felt dimensions of movement" that she persuasively argues, "opens the way for an examination of kinetic vitality as an overlooked aspect of embodied knowledge."[50]

Additionally, whilst participating in such ritual, some of the younger people attending have made use of my camera to take photos and film me, perhaps a strategy to have proof of the event, or evidence of my unusual presence "there." Sarah Pink discusses in her book on visual ethnography[51] how ethnographers in the field have been known to use the photos of themselves in the field to convince the reader of an authoritative voice—of the authenticity of really "being there." As she states, "We can see the camera as another aspect of the ethnographer's emplacement, and as such, as part of the entanglement of place."[52] Yet here in this example the tables are turned and it becomes a strategy of my informants, recording the presence of the non-Hindu, emplaced, and participating fully in their

---

[48] Johannes Fabian, Time and the Work of Anthropology: Critical Essays 1971-1991 (Reading and Paris: Harwood Academic Publishers, 1991), 264.

[49] Nabhan-Warren, 401.

[50] Deidre Sklar, "Remembering Kinesthesia: an Inquiry into Embodied Cultural Knowledge," in Migrations of Gesture, eds. Carrie Noland and Sally Ann Ness (Minneapolis and London: University of Minnesota Press, 2008), 85.

[51] Sarah Pink, Doing Visual Ethnography: Images, Media and Representation in Research (London: Sage Publications, 2001), 122.

[52] Pink, Doing Sensory Ethnography, 100.

religious, devotional ritual. An illustration of how, as Peter Collins stresses, the ethnographic self is a resource—in this case, the self of the ethnographer is drawn upon by others, and is treated as a resource by them.[53] It underlines too, the very embodied nature of fieldwork, of bodily participation in activity, regardless of whether one is dancing or not. Anthropologist Judith Oakley writes how "Making sense of fieldwork is a bodily process"[54] and further remarks that "Knowing others through the instrument of the field worker's own body involves deconstructing the body as a cultural, biographical construction through a lived and interactive encounter with others' cultural construction and bodily experience."[55] It is a kinaesthetic and sensual process.

The following two examples from my ethnographic fieldwork are of traditional dance performances that are to all appearances, non-participatory. I begin with the Indian classical dance style of Bharatanatyam, performed at the autumn festival of *Navratri* by Tamil youngsters, again in a religious setting, in the Shri Mahalakshmi Temple in East Ham, East London.[56] Because of its context of performance, it is not possible for the audience to join in this religious danced presentation by non-professional but highly trained, young dancers. But for both the ethnographer and the audience, a certain cultural competence brings a level of understanding and a type, I would suggest, of cultural intimacy, perhaps even of a level of performative involvement. My own training in this classical dance style brings an intimate and bodily understanding of gestures, steps, positions, rhythms and dance terminology as well as of the myths and religious stories that are being portrayed. I have learnt some of the items performed and I am familiar with some of the songs and the music being used. The audience of devotees in the temple partakes of a cultural competence in differing levels, as engaged spectators, and as religious followers who know the stories and music. Added to this is the interest of migrant parents to see their daughters performing a classical dance style, as scholar Ketu Katrak point outs, "For immigrants, especially first-generation parents, the dance is a repository of cultural knowledge to be imparted to their children...Dance, as inscribed on the body through Bharata Natyam gestures, embodies Indian culture, which is a complex and diverse arena more tangible than cultural artifacts that can be transported into relocated

[53] Collins, 16.
[54] Judith Oakley, "Fieldwork Embodied," The Sociological Review 55, no. 1 (2007): 77.
[55] Ibid., 77.
[56] See David, "Performing for the Gods."

homes."[57] The complexities that abound in this devoutly Hindu performative
arena relating to the dance's history in India and its expulsion from the
temples form too large a debate to be entered upon here. They also have
been well rehearsed by other scholars[58] but in this setting, remain
relatively unquestioned by those present in the audience. For me as
ethnographer, whilst not being physically embodied in the dance at that
time of performance, previous bodily experience brings a deeper level of
understanding of the nuances, context, history and performative layers
shown here.

Context, history and performance brings us to the final illustration
taken from very recent fieldwork in a new area of my research relating to
the *'Cham* ritual dances of the monks of Bhutan, who practise Tibetan
Buddhism, based on Indian Vajrayana (Tantric) Buddhism. I raise it here,
as part of this chapter's enquiry into embodied ethnography, as I am trying
to discover how, in a situation where participatory performance is not
allowed (as a lay, non-Buddhist woman), one might still try to find, and
possibly experience that "interior" embodied knowledge. Whilst in Bhutan
in January 2012, we made a complete filmed documentation of the dances
of the 3-day religious festival (*tsechu*) in the Bhutanese town of Trongsa.
Each dance has a fairly long duration (1-2 hours), is performed by monks
and is integral to the religious ritual. The dances at this festival were
watched by an audience of approximately 600-700 people of all ages, and
the particular dance I am discussing is the Tantric *Tungam 'cham*, the
"Dance of the Fearsome Deities." History and mythology, as well as
religion are at the heart of this traditional annual *tsechu* in central Bhutan.
The three-day event draws crowds of local people, eager to watch the all-
day dancing, converse, socialise, buy from local traders, as well as to gain
spiritual merit from attending the long, didactic and Tantric dance dramas
performed by the resident monks and occasionally some village male
dancers. Set in one of the three courtyards of a medieval fortress, called a
dzong that is home to the large monastery and the seat of local government

---

[57] Ketu Katrak, "The Gestures of Bharata Natyam: Migrating into Diasporic
Contemporary Indian Dance," in Migrations of Gesture, eds. Carrie Noland and
Sally Ann Ness (Minneapolis and London: University of Minnesota Press, 2008),
221.
[58] Avanthi Meduri, "Bharatanatyam as World Historical Form," in Bharatanatyam:
A Reader, ed. Davesh Soneji (New Delhi: Oxford University Press, 2010), 253-
273; Amrit Srivinasan, "Reform and Revival: the Devadasi and Her Dance,"
Economic and Political weekly XX, no. 44 (1985): 1869-1876; O'Shea, "Dancing
Through History."

administration, the monks' traditional *'Cham* dances create a physical, external pattern of their inner meditations, whirling, jumping and stepping in rhythmic cycles. As many writers have pointed out[59] these ritual dances, seen all over the Himalayan region in their generic form, as well as their particular manifestations that are local and specific, carry layers of embodied religious, Tantric and transformative meaning. Indeed, the written text of the 5th Dalai Lama on the dance of 1650 specifically indicates "Every movement has a significance."[60] Additionally, there appear to be two major sequences within all the many types of *'Cham* dance—firstly that of marking and defining (and cleansing) the ground as sacred space[61] using stamping steps such as "the thunderbolt step," and the ritual destruction of the *linga*, the sign or receptacle of evil forces.

Now, as a dance ethnographer, I question how one might begin to understand the complexities of the movement forms utilised here. Leaving to one side interviews with the monks and their teachers (a process which has started, but has to be continued) there are one or two options that could be taken forward. Firstly I was able to film complete dances being performed in two very different festival settings, and secondly, had the privilege to watch and film a group of monks in rehearsal, and out of costume. In order to begin to analyse the movement, I have watched a selection of the movement sequences in these films at slow speed. I will then learn these danced components to enable a more embodied sense of the different danced components—the transference of body weight, the rotation of the upper body and whole form in the complete turns, as well as an understanding of the exaggerated upper body movements in which the dancers bend down from the waist to the left and to the right, lean down frontwards towards their feet and also execute extended back bends. These rotations and bending of the spine are some of the most memorable sequences in the 2 hour-long dances, as are the whirling turns, performed using different dynamics of speed. Turning is repeated on one side, and then almost as if unwinding, on the other. The right foot is picked up and a

---

[59] See Cathy Cantwell, "The Dance of the Guru's Eight Aspects," Cathy Cantwell, http://ngb.csac.anthropology.ac.uk/csac/NGB/Doc_ext/Gar.xml (accessed January 10, 2012); Matthieu Ricard, Monk Dancers of Tibet (Boston and London: Shambala, 2003); Geoffrey Samuel, Tantric Revisionings: New Understandings of Tibetan Buddhism and Indian Religion (Delhi and London: Motilal Banarsidass and Ashgate, 2005; Mona Schrempf, "Tibetan Ritual Dances and the Transformation of Space," Tibet International 19, no. 2 (1994): 95-120.
[60] Cantwell, "The Dance."
[61] Schrempf, op.cit.

hopping turn, in place, is made to the left. This is followed by jumping and
stepped turns in the same direction. The dancer repeats this to the left, a
type of repetition of the circularity. Deep bends of the upper body, forward
and back, and along the diagonal, are made in between the turns, with the
weight of the head leading the body as it orbits around the anchor of the
midpoint of the body, like a central axis. The monk dancers create circles
in the space, produce circles around one another and make a type of
melodic circle in the body itself, all this emphasizing the important
Mandala pattern. The concentration of power is directed towards the
centre of the circle, and here in the *Tungam cham* at this Bhutanese *tsechu*,
the power is a destructive one, as the *linga* will be ritually killed. The
linga additionally represents the notion of ego, or the internal and external
obstacles to spiritual progress,[62] which itself has to be subdued for spiritual
enlightenment to take place. Movements advance and retreat, open and
close, rise and fall.[63] Some of the whirling movements in other dances at
the same ritual event remind one of the deeply meditative and devotional
turning of the Sufi dervishes, where fast whirling of the body, in place,
and moving slowly in circular fashion, is believed to dissolve ego and
allow a meditation on the divine. In Vajrayana Buddhism, visualisation in
meditation is a key practice in becoming, or taking on aspects of the deity,
and there is no doubt that some parts of this are being embodied and
displayed in such ritual dances. All of this indicates the need for thorough
research through contextual study in addition to observation and any
amount of bodily practice that might be possible.

To conclude, I would like to note here how previous and current work
taking place in the development of the anthropology of the senses supports
the notion of the embodied ethnographer. Paul Stoller's writing in the late
1990's,[64] followed by many other anthropologists, some specifically
working in dance such as Hahn,[65] Skinner[66] and Yolanda van Ede[67]

---

[62] See Cathy Cantwell, "To Meditate upon Consciousness as *Vajra*: Ritual 'killing
and liberation' in the Rnying-ma-pa Tradition," Tibetan Studies 1, (1997): 107-
118.
[63] Terms used in Laban Movement Analysis (LMA).
[64] Paul Stoller, Sensuous Scholarship (Philadelphia: University of Pennsylvania
Press, 1997).
[65] Hahn, op.cit.
[66] Skinner, op. cit.
[67] Yolanda van Ede, "Sounding Contestation, Silent Suppression: Cosmopolitics
and Gender in Japanese Flamenco, in Politics of Embodiment: Dance and Identities

discuss how embodied practice on the part of the ethnographer allows an understanding of the most profound type of knowledge which is often not spoken.[68] These academics/practitioners confirm how engaging with the senses yields a different understanding of space, place and time. Such work on movement forms through the anthropology of the senses also reveals the necessity for researchers to suspend western epistemological approaches and hierarchies in their analysis. This may allow for a discovery of alternative sites of knowledge that do not privilege, for example, the sight, or the written text that have always been the mainstays of anthropological participant observation. Skinner in fact argues for the need for "bodynotes" in fieldwork, as opposed to the ethnographer's usual "headnotes."[69] Sklar records how "in dance scholarship, both aesthetic and historical studies tend to display a visualist bias, even though the primary media of dancing is movement."[70] Several of these theorists write of needing to learn to "listen to embodiment," or to hear "the voice of the body,"[71] indicating a level of understanding and connection that is perhaps normally concealed.

The fieldwork examples cited engage with a variety of types of "traditional performance" and in discussing them, I have questioned how engaged, emplaced ethnography might allow us, in differing ways, to watch, feel and experience; to listen to the body and understand through the body whatever movement practice is under consideration. In some cases, full participation in movement practices is possible, in others one's involvement is partial and in some examples, there appears to be no possibility of overt engagement at all. Yet to return to Geertz's words, "being there" as ethnographer in terms of performance, seems to me to be about embodying the movement in whatever way might be feasible. Through this, one is empowered to transcend the usual limits of understanding, using phenomenological knowledge to challenge the more orthodox forms of cognition and perception. This quote from philosopher Michel Foucault highlights the need to extend our thinking and our knowledge in such ways:

---

in a Globalized World, eds. Ann R. David and Linda Dankworth (Basingstoke, Hants: Palgrave Macmillan, 2013): forthcoming.

[68] Pink, *Doing Sensory Ethnography*.

[69] Skinner, "Leading Questions," 120.

[70] Sklar, "Remembering Kinesthesia," 88.

[71] Nabhan-Warren, 388.

There are times in life when the question of knowing if one can think differently than one thinks, and perceive differently than one sees, is absolutely necessary if one is to go on looking and reflecting at all...But, then, what is philosophy today—philosophical activity, I mean—if it is not the critical work that thought brings to bear on itself? In what does it consist, if not in the endeavor to know how and to what extent it might be possible to think differently, instead of legitimizing what is already known?[72]

The agentive, lived experience of the body in dance, of its primacy in place raises some deeply philosophical questions and ontological perspectives.[73] This chapter has engaged with some of those questions, leaving others open for further pursuit. Many of these issues remain elusive and need to be approached again and again, from differing standpoints and interdisciplinary frameworks. Juxtapositions highlighted by sociologists Helen Thomas and Jamila Ahmed such as "the researcher's body is immersed in the field and is simultaneously outside the research (by means of its strangeness and lack of knowledge) and in the research (by the fact of its physical presence)"[74] indicate the complexity and richness of the emplaced body as a tool for ethnographic research. All these factors open up new trajectories for thinking and moving and the possibility of "new moments of knowing."[75]

Work Cited

Amit, Vered, ed. *Constructing the Field: Ethnographic Fieldwork in the Contemporary World.* London: Routledge, 2000.
Blacking, John. *How Musical is Man?* Seattle and London: University of Washington Press, 1973.
Buckland, Theresa, ed. *Dance in the Field: Theory, Methods and Issues in Dance Ethnography.* Basingstoke, UK: Macmillan Press, 1999.

---

[72] Michel Foucault, The History of Sexuality, vol. 2, Trans. Robert Hurley (London: Penguin, 1987), 8-9.
[73] Sally Ann Ness, "Being a Body in a Cultural Way: Understanding the Cultural in the Embodiment of Dance," in Cultural Bodies: Ethnography and Theory, eds. Helen Thomas and Jamila Ahmed, 123-144 (Oxford: Blackwell Publishing, 2004).
[74] Helen Thomas and Jamila Ahmed, eds., Cultural Bodies: Ethnography and Theory (Oxford: Blackwell Publishing, 2004), 3.
[75] Halstead, "Introduction," 7.

Buckland, Theresa. "Dance, Authenticity and Cultural Memory: the Politics of Embodiment." *Yearbook for Traditional Music* 33, (2001): 1-16.

Buckland, Theresa, ed. *Dancing from Past to Present. Nation, Culture, Identities.* Wisconsin: University of Wisconsin Press, 2006.

Cantwell, Cathy. "To Meditate upon Consciousness as *Vajra:* Ritual 'killing and liberation' in the Rnying-ma-pa Tradition." *Tibetan Studies* 1, (1997): 107-118.

Cantwell, Cathy. "The Dance of the Guru's Eight Aspects." Cantwell, Cathy. Last Modified 2003.
http://ngb.csac.anthropology.ac.uk/csac/NGB/Doc_ext/Gar.xml.

Collins, Peter, ed. *The Ethnographic Self as Resource: Writing Memory and Experience into Ethnography.* Oxford and New York: Berghahn Books, 2010.

Daboo, Jerri. *Ritual, Rapture and Remorse: a study of Tarantism and Pizzica in Salento.* Oxford: Peter Lang, 2010.

David, Ann R. "Local Diasporas/Global Trajectories: New Aspects of Religious 'Performance' in British Tamil Hindu Practice." *Performance Research* 13, no. 3 (2008): 89-99.

—. "Performing for the Gods? Dance and Embodied Ritual in British Hindu Temples." *South Asian Popular Culture* 7, no. 3 (2009): 217-231.

—. "Gendering the Divine: New Forms of Feminine Hindu Worship." *International Journal of Hindu Studies* 13, no. 3 (2010): 337-55.

—. "Sacralising the City: Sound, Space and Performance in Hindu Ritual Practices in London." *Special issue: Culture & Religion* 13, no. 4 (2012): 449-467.

—. "Embodied traditions: Gujarati (dance) Practices of *garba* and *raas* in the UK Context" In *Politics of Embodiment: Dance and Identities in a Globalized World*, edited by Ann R. David and Linda Dankworth. Basingstoke, Hants: Palgrave Macmillan, 2013 (forthcoming).

Denzin, Norman K. *Performance Ethnography. Critical Pedagogy and the Politics of Culture.* Thousand Oaks; London; New Delhi: Sage Publications, 2003.

Fabian, Johannes. *Time and the Work of Anthropology: Critical Essays 1971-1991.* Reading and Paris: Harwood Academic Publishers, 1991.

Farnell, Brenda. "It Goes Without Saying—But Not Always." In *Dance in the Field: Theory, Methods and Issues in Dance Ethnography*, edited by Theresa Buckland, 145-160. Basingstoke, UK: Macmillan Press, 1999.

Foucault, Michel. *The History of Sexuality, vol. 2*. Trans. Robert Hurley. London: Penguin, 1987.

Geertz, Clifford. *Works and Lives: The Anthropologist as Author*. Stanford, California: Stanford University Press, 1988.

—. *Available Light: Anthropological Reflections on Philosophic Topics.* Princeton and Oxford: Princeton University Press, 2000.

Grau, Andrée. "John Blacking and the Development of Dance Anthropology in the United Kingdom." *Dance Research Journal* 25, no. 2 (1993): 21-31

—. "Fieldwork, Politics and Power." In *Dance in the Field: Theory, Methods and Issues in Dance Ethnography*, edited by Theresa Buckland, 163-174. Basingstoke, UK: Macmillan Press, 1999.

—. "Tiwi Dance Aesthetics." *Yearbook for Traditional Music* 35, (2003): 175-180.

—. "Dance, Anthropology, and Research through Practice." Paper presented at the CORD conference, Paris France, 2007, 1-5.

Hahn, Tomie. *Sensational Knowledge: Embodying Culture through Japanese Dance*. Middletown, Conn: Wesleyan University Press, 2007.

Halstead, Narmala. "Introduction. Experiencing the Ethnographic Present: Knowing through 'Crisis.'" In *Knowing How to Know. Fieldwork and the Ethnographic Present,* edited by Narmala Halstead and others, 1-21. New York and Oxford: Berghahn Books, 2008.

Halstead, Narmala and others, eds. *Knowing How to Know. Fieldwork and the Ethnographic Present*. New York and Oxford: Berghahn Books, 2008.

Hood, Mantle. "The Challenge of 'Bi-musicality.'" *Ethnomusicology* 4, no. 2 (1960): 55-59.

Hughes-Freeland, Felicia. "Dance on Film: Strategy and Serendipity." In *Dance in the Field: Theory, Methods and Issues in Dance Ethnography,* edited by Theresa Buckland, 111-122. Basingstoke: Macmillan Press, 1999.

Katrak, Ketu. "The Gestures of Bharata Natyam: Migrating into Diasporic Contemporary Indian Dance." In *Migrations of Gesture*, edited by Carrie Noland and Sally Ann Ness, 217-240. Minneapolis and London: University of Minnesota Press, 2008.

McNeill, William H. *Keeping Together in Time: Dance and Drill in Human History*. Cambridge, MA: Harvard University Press, 1995.

Meduri, Avanthi. "Bharatanatyam as World Historical Form." In *Bharatanatyam: A Reader*, edited by Davesh Soneji, 253-273. New Delhi: Oxford University Press, 2010.

Nabhan-Warren, Kirsty. "Embodied Research and Writing: A Case for Phenomenologically Oriented Religious Studies Ethnographies." *Journal of the American Academy of Religion* 79, no. 2 (2011): 378-407.

Ness, Sally Ann. *Body, Movement, and Culture: Kinesthetic and Visual Symbolism in a Philippine Community.* Philadelphia: University of Pennsylvania Press, 1992.

—. "Being a Body in a Cultural Way: Understanding the Cultural in the Embodiment of Dance." In *Cultural Bodies. Ethnography and Theory,* edited by Helen Thomas and Jamila Ahmed, 123-144. Oxford: Blackwell Publishing, 2004.

Oakley, Judith. "Fieldwork Embodied." *The Sociological Review* 55, vol. 1 (2007): 65-79.

O'Shea, Janet. "Dancing through History and Ethnography: Indian Classical Dance and the Performance of the Past." In *Dancing from Past to Present. Nation, Culture, Identities*, edited by Theresa Buckland, 123-152. Wisconsin: University of Wisconsin Press, 2006.

Pink, Sarah. *Doing Visual Ethnography: Images, Media and Representation in Research.* London: Sage Publications, 2001.

—. *Doing Sensory Ethnography.* London: Sage Publications, 2009.

Phillips-Silver, Jessica and others. "The Ecology of Entrainment: Foundations of Coordinated Rhythmic Movement." *Music Perception: An Interdisciplinary Journal* 28, no. 1 (2010): 3-14.

Ranmarine, Tina K. "Performance and Experiential Learning in the Study of Ethnomusicology." In *Learning Fields: Current Policies and Practices in European Social Anthropology Education,* edited by Dorie Drackle and Iain Edgar, 227-240. Oxford and New York: Berghahn Books, 2004.

Ricard, Matthieu. *Monk Dancers of Tibet.* Boston and London: Shambala, 2003.

Samuel Geoffrey. *Tantric Revisionings: New Understandings of Tibetan Buddhism and Indian Religion.* Delhi and London: Motilal Banarsidass and Ashgate, 2005.

Schrempf, Mona. "Tibetan Ritual Dances and the Transformation of Space." *Tibet International* 19, no. 2 (1994): 95-120.

Skinner, Jonathan. "Leading Questions and Body Memories: a Case of Phenomenology and Physical Ethnography in the Dance Interview." In *The Ethnographic Self as Resource: Writing Memory and Experience into Ethnography*, edited by Peter Collins, 111-128. Oxford and New York: Berghahn Books, 2010.

Sklar, Deidre. "On Dance Ethnography." *Dance Research Journal* 23, (1991): 6-10.
—. *Dancing with the Virgin: Body and Faith in the Fiesta of Tortugas, New Mexico.* Berkeley, California: University of California Press, 2001.
—. "Remembering Kinesthesia: an Inquiry into Embodied Cultural Knowledge." In *Migrations of Gesture*, edited by Carrie Noland and Sally Ann Ness, 85-111. Minneapolis and London: University of Minnesota Press, 2008.
Srinivasan, Amrit. "Reform and Revival: The Devadasi and Her Dance." *Economic and Political Weekly* XX, no. 44 (1985): 1869-1876.
Stoller, Paul. *Sensuous Scholarship.* Philadelphia: University of Pennsylvania Press, 1997.
Strathern, Marilyn. *Property, Substance and Effect: Anthropological Essays on Persons and Things.* London: Athlone Press, 1999.
Thomas, Helen and Jamila Ahmed, eds. *Cultural Bodies. Ethnography and Theory*. Oxford: Blackwell Publishing, 2004.
Titon, Jeff Todd. "Bi-Musicality as Metaphor," *The Journal of American Folklore* 108, no. 429 (1995): 287-297.
Tweed, Thomas. *Crossing and Dwelling: A Theory of Religion.* Boston: Harvard University Press, 2006.
Van Ede, Yolanda. "Sounding Contestation, Silent Suppression Cosmopolitics and Gender in Japanese Flamenco." In *Politics of Embodiment: Dance and Identities in a Globalized World,* edited by Ann R. David and Linda Dankworth. Basingstoke, Hants: Palgrave Macmillan, 2013 (forthcoming).

CHAPTER FOUR

THE ARTISANAL INSTRUMENT MAKER IN THE MOMENT OF PERFORMANCE: MOTIVATION AND MEANING IN THE SCOTTISH SMALLPIPES REVIVAL

BENJAMIN POWER

My research, and this chapter, engages artisanal instrument makers and their craft. I have sought to explore the motivations of such makers and to explain why they produce both the general types and the particular instruments that they do (even why they make them at all) and to understand the effects of their labours on musicians, performance and tradition. This exploration has seemed to require the synthesis of some sort of theory to integrate the labour of the instrument maker with that of the musician, and which would comprehend the interleaved motivations behind the whole. This chapter, then, attempts to develop such an approach and does so by moving toward an understanding of performance that is exemplified by artisanal instrument making. This type of performance is initially of an individual sort that takes place around the process of manufacture, but it is subsequently of a compound character, combining the initial performance of the makers with that of the musicians who play their instruments. My understanding of it knits together theories of performance drawn from three disciplines; utopian performance from Jill Dolan (theatre studies), performance through material culture from Henry Glassie (folklore), and the demonstration of value in performance from Paul Eiss (anthropology).

The particular example of this chapter is that of the recent reinvention and vigorous revival of bellows driven bagpipes in Scotland—pipes designed for playing indoors and with other instruments. The change wrought in Scottish piping by this revival has been driven in no small way by artisanal instrument makers and their interaction with both existing and

new traditions of music making. Moreover, because the bagpipes in
Scotland are an iconic national symbol, this change is inextricably linked
to issues of Scottish identity.

Iain MacInnes, a celebrated piper, producer, and academic, asserts that
the revival of bellows driven bagpipes in Scotland may have reached its
end, in that such instruments are once again "an established feature of the
Scottish musical landscape."[1] The "once again" speaks to the fact that
until 150 years ago there were several types of bagpipe in Scotland for
instance small indoor bagpipes, which can be found in many museums.[2]
Yet between the middle of the nineteenth-century and the early 1980's,
museums were just about the only place in Scotland where they might be
found with any consistency. This state of affairs, that the only surviving
bagpipe in Scotland was the Great Highland Bagpipe (hereafter the GHB,
the great pipes or the highland pipes), arose from the destruction of the
clan system and highland society after the Acts of Union between Scotland
and England of 1706-7, the two subsequent failed Jacobite rebellions, and
the Highland clearances that followed.[3] These events, among others,
largely destroyed the population that had supported bagpipes in Scotland,
and even the highland pipes themselves were only saved because of their
suitability (ferocious volume and affordance of display) for adoption by
the British military as it raised its highland regiments. This adoption was
followed by the instrument's promotion by Highland Societies, which
hoped to construct a new Scottish identity within Britain, and which,
adopting the highland pipes as a national symbol, ran competitions in

---

[1] Iain MacInnes, "Taking Stock: Lowland and Border Piping in a Highland
World," in The Highland Bagpipe: Music, History, Tradition, ed. Joshua Dickson
(Aldershot: Ashgate, 2009), 188.
[2] Hugh Cheape, Bagpipes: A National Collection of a National Treasure
(Edinburgh: National Museums of Scotland, 2007).
[3] The Acts of Union were passed in 1706 and 1707 by the parliaments of England
and Scotland respectively. They united the two countries as one, Great Britain,
under a single parliament. Two Jacobite rebellions followed, in 1715 and 1745,
heavily supported by highland clans, which aimed to restore the Stuart kings. Each
failed, and because of their support of the Stuarts, the clans and their culture were
targeted by the Hanoverian government. The demise of the clan system was
followed by the highland clearances which took place in the late 18th and 19th
centuries and were a Scottish occurrence of land enclosure. Landowners, supported
by the state, removed the large highland population of tenant farmers from their
crofts in a process of forced migration, often to Cape Breton Island in Canada, and
replaced them with more lucrative sheep.

which military pipers mainly competed.[4] This dual influence, of the military pipe band and the competition, led the highland piping tradition to become stylised, regimented, heavily literate, proscribed and highly technically accomplished. At the time that Scottish bellows pipes were reintroduced in the 1980's, it was the sole piping tradition in Scotland, extremely strong, and arguably "classical" in its practice. That these smaller bagpipes have once again become "an established feature of the Scottish musical landscape," is, then, an extraordinary turnaround, particularly, it would seem, because of the dominant position of the Great Highland Bagpipe and its very particular tradition which might be supposed to be resistant to such encroachment. Yet it has taken only a quarter century to reestablish them in regular production following a century and a half of near extinction.

Writing predominantly for the aforementioned Highland piping tradition audience, MacInnes points to the major reason for the Scottish smallpipes' remarkable success:

> ...we have genuine revival, mixed with more than a hint of reinvention. No one would claim that the low-pitch smallpipes which dominated the early years of the revival have much in common with eighteenth-century instruments, but they have nonetheless helped foster a climate in which Highland pipers can take to the bellows with ease, and enjoy the instrument without totally relearning technique and repertoire.[5]

These pipes, which were the first type of bagpipe produced in the Scottish bellows pipes revival, share the same scale and fingering as their larger and louder cousin and are thus playable using much of the same technique. They make use of the strength and breadth of the Highland pipe tradition, and it is Highland pipers that make up the majority of those who are now playing them. This is by design: Robert Greensitt, a pioneering smallpipe maker, contends that "modern small pipes are unashamedly made with Highland pipers and a Highland repertoire in mind."[6] This was certainly the case in the 1970's and early 1980's when many of the

---

[4] John H. Gibson, Traditional Gaelic Bagpiping, 1745-1945 (Montreal: McGill-Queen's University Press, 1998); see also Iain MacInnes, The Highland Bagpipe: The Impact of the Highland Societies of London and Scotland, 1781-1844 (Edinburgh: University of Edinburgh, 1989).
[5] MacInnes, "Taking Stock," 188.
[6] Robert Greensitt. "Letters," Common Stock: The Journal of the Lowland and the Borders Piper's Society 7, no. 1 (1992): 3.

individuals who were driving forces in the revival played the great pipes themselves. By way of example, these were the people who approached pipemaker Colin Ross (a Northumbrian pipemaker popularly considered as the inventor of the modern instrument) with requests for some sort of "small Scottish bagpipe."

So these modern Scottish smallpipes are instruments that, bellows aside, are played the same way as the Highland pipes, but why would such numbers of highland pipers wish to play them? The answer is that they immediately redress a fundamental quality of the Highland pipes that is a significant disadvantage in a number of areas: their volume—smallpipes are very much quieter and lend themselves to being played both indoors and with other instruments. This provides pipers with a new outlet for the practice and performance of existing technique and repertoire. It was this existing constituency of pipers with a predisposition to the new instrument that prompted the beginning of regular production. Hamish Moore, a grade 1 competition piper, was one of the first to begin making these smallpipes full time.

> These developments, given the number of Highland pipers in the world, created a commercially viable situation for the many fledgling pipe-makers who were to start making these pipes professionally.[7]

Yet the economic viability that tied the makers of the new pipes to the existing pipe tradition was in contradiction to the cultural ambitions of many of the prime movers in the bellows pipes' revival. The first institution to champion the new instrument was the Lowland and Border Pipers' Society (hereafter the LBPS). Moore and the other founders of the Society such as Hugh Cheape, a curator with the National Museums of Scotland (then the National Museum of Antiquities of Scotland), did not intend these new instruments to become simply a quieter echo of their much larger, louder and well-established brethren:

> Curiosity and conviction drove the Society to question received opinion and the hegemony of the Great Highland Bagpipe in the musical culture of Scotland. It may be that the time was ripe for change and that the culture of piping, as represented by the solo and pipe band competitions, was

---

[7] Hamish Moore, "National Museum of Scotland Craft Exhibition Essay," www.hamishmoore.com, http://hamishmoore.com/essays.htm#intro (accessed May 19, 2009).

experiencing diminishing returns of public interest and reaching limits of evolution.[8]

Moore, among others, had become particularly dissatisfied with the state of the Scottish piping tradition by the beginning of the 1980's. He argued, in letters to *Common Stock, the Journal of the Lowland and Border Pipers' Society*, as well as in liner notes to his various recordings, that,

> piping was, in Scotland, prior to the British Army recruiting the Highland regiments and the advent of competition, wild and vigorous with individual styles existing, [and, furthermore] that competitions have in fact encouraged technical correctness to the detriment of musicality.[9]

It was this older style of Scottish music which he found preserved in Cape Breton Island, Nova Scotia, an enclave of Scottish culture, which was played in a much more sociable context than contemporary Highland piping, and he hoped to revive it once more in Scotland.

According to Moore, it was the social and political history of Scotland since the eighteen-century that had led to the status quo in highland piping, along with the aforementioned decline in other types of bagpipes:

> We need only look at the social and political history of the country and its direct effect on the culture—Culloden and the Act of Proscription;[10] the Highland Clearances; the Church who were responsible for burning vast numbers of fiddles... the Victorianisation of Scotland... the successive waves of English and European fashion in dancing; the overwhelming influence which competition and the army had on piping.[11]

---

[8] Hugh Cheape, "'Happy We've Been a' Thegither:' New Directions in Piping," Common Stock: The Journal of the Lowland and the Borders Pipers' Society 23, no. 2 (2008): 12.

[9] Hamish Moore, "Stepping on the Bridge," Audio CD, Original Edition, Greentrax Records, CDTRAX073, East Lothian, (1994): liner notes, 6.

[10] Culloden was the site of the final, and for the Jacobite cause catastrophic, battle of the 1745 Scottish rebellion. The 1746 Act of Proscription followed the suppression of the rebellion and forbade the wearing of highland dress or the bearing of arms in an attempt to end the clan system in Scotland and the likelihood of further rebellion. The highland clearances took place in the late eighteenth and nineteenth centuries after the fall of the clan system. Landowners replaced the large highland population of tenant farmers with more lucrative sheep, forcing them in most cases to emigrate or starve.

[11] Moore, "Stepping On," 3.

Yet it was not only such chronologically distant injustices that moved Moore and various other members of the then embryonic LBPS; contemporary politics and society were and are equally influential. The various historical discourses Moore mentioned, among others more recent, gave rise to a rebellious political climate in Scotland under the Conservative governments of Margaret Thatcher and John Major. These were so spectacularly unpopular they failed to win a single Scottish parliamentary seat in the 1997 general election. In a letter to *Common Stock* detailing his resignation in 1993, Andy Hunter, an LBPS committee member, spoke of the society's importance in this respect:

> The Society, in the same way as any other cultural body in Scotland at the present time, is in the forefront of a vital struggle, whether it likes it or not. Our national aspirations have been ground down by 14 years of alien rule… In the near future, all we will be left with will be our culture. I am firmly convinced that every facet of our national culture will soon be called upon to bear a considerable load as the search for identity and self-esteem continues.[12]

For others, such as the piper and researcher Matt Seattle, it was contemporary mass cultural icons that were the "common enemy" which "pipers from all nations should be… uniting against."[13] For these musicians, the pipes that Moore (among other makers) made and makes in accordance with his own ideology of community music making—musicking of a type that last existed in piping circles prior to the Highland Clearances—change the possible cultural meanings of the bagpipes. Bellows blown pipes made by Moore and his contemporaries afford them, as they see it, a way to resist hegemonic power of one sort or other—a regretted historical discourse, the power of an uncaring and foreign state, or the depredations of commodified, mass-mediatized culture—even in the moment of their own musical performance.

This chapter sets out to discuss the manner in which the ideas of an instrument maker are congealed in his instruments which in turn carry them forward to the moment of performance by musicians such as Andy Hunter and Matt Seattle. I make the argument that the construction of a musical instrument can be usefully understood, in a manner more than

---

[12] Andy Hunter, "Letters," Common Stock: The Journal of the Lowland and Borders Pipers' Society 8, no. 2 (1993): 4.
[13] Matt Seattle, "Letters," Common Stock: The Journal of the Lowland and Borders Pipers' Society 9, no. 1 (1994): 4.

simply metaphorical, as performance. That same instrument, in the immediate and drastic moment in which it is played, becomes an enabling and simultaneously limiting aspect of a second performance—that of the musician. This second performance is born of the overlapping intentions of maker and player. An instrument's qualities are most frequently ascribed to the artifact itself rather than to the social relations that give rise to it, and in this process the influence of the instrument maker is marginalized, overlooked in general and under-theorised in the academy. I attempt to address the following questions: Can the instrument maker be said to be somehow present in the moment of performance? What part does the instrument maker take in the performance of the musician? How does this influence connect to his initial motivations for producing the instruments that he does?

Creation (and the Performance of Value)

It may be doubted whether instrument making is, in truth, performance. Whether some act *is* a performance is, as Richard Schechner points out, contingent upon convention and tradition. However, almost all acts, he goes on to stress, can be studied *as* performance, that is, as the process of performance.[14] In this section of the paper I argue that engaging artisanal instrument making and its connection to subsequent music making may facilitate a more nuanced understanding of it as process. It is this approach that features in the work of folklorists such as Henry Glassie. In his book *Material Culture,* Glassie centers his method of inquiry around the artifact as text, though he is careful to attach the word text to its original meaning: something *woven* out of other things.[15] He explains that artifacts as texts must be examined in multiple contexts, and that they thus accrue layer upon layer of meaning for the observer.

Glassie groups the myriad contexts in which an artifact moves into three "master" contexts, those of creation, communication, and consumption, each of which may be understood in light of performance.[16] As Kara Lochridge has argued, this sort of analysis is particularly rewarding in the case of artisanal instruments because, firstly, each individual instrument is

---

[14] Richard Schechner, Performance Studies: An Introduction (London: Routledge, 2002), 30.
[15] Henry Glassie, Material Culture (Bloomington: Indiana University Press, 1999), 45.
[16] Ibid., 48.

a single maker's vision, and secondly, each instrument is necessarily and immediately implicated in affording very conventional types of subsequent musical performance.[17] That is, the manner in which an instrument is constructed, particularly if that construction is of singular design, dramatically affects the music that is subsequently played upon it. Thus, an examination of these two actions, musical instrument production and musical performance as performative processes of, respectively, creation and consumption, permits a comparison of each performer's motivations and their interaction, locating the maker in the moment of musical performance.

In the first of Glassie's contexts, creation, the artisan pipemaker transfers himself, his ideas, and his ideology into the artifact as he designs and makes it through a performative process. Though this process must necessarily produce a distinct instrument, the individuality of the work and therefore its particular impact on subsequent performance is likely to be the greater when an instrument is at an unstable period in its development. We can see and hear this in the remarkable variety of the bellows blown pipes currently in production, and particularly in the case of the Scottish border pipe—the second type of bagpipe of Scotland's bellows pipe revival. Differences between instruments may be remarkable. One instrument called a Scottish border pipe may be quite different in timbre, volume, intonation or appearance from another precisely because one maker's understanding of it may be quite different from his colleague's.

According to Glassie the artisan engages in an act of creation which both reaches back and projects forward. Hamish Moore, for example, engages with memory in multiple ways. His virtuosic musicianship, his experience of competition piping, his dissatisfaction with competitive contexts, his past hope and desires for a perfect instrument, his accumulated technical skill as a craftsman and instrument maker. Projecting forward there is the prospect of economic viability, the anticipation of the instrument being played, the intent the instrument may carry, the ideas and meanings he has placed in it. All of these are informed by his knowledge of history as it intertwines with his present political view.

In the example of Hamish Moore and the Scottish smallpipes, this context of historical consideration is particularly important, because it was

---

[17] Kara Lochridge, "'Where Can I Get a Flute Like Yours?:' Art and Material Culture in the Irish Flute Tradition" (PhD diss., University of Indiana, 2005), 127.

this that offered him a clear avenue of change; an alternative to the musical tradition and the instrument he was accustomed to play. This can be understood in more depth in light of Paul Eiss' contention that value can be observed in performance.[18] Seeing Moore's instrument making as a form of performance is a way to shed light on his perception of history and its connection to his ideas of value, all of which, taken together, explain his motivation to make the instruments (both the type and the individual examples) that he does. Eiss uses the idea of performance as process to account for the value that people place upon objects, suggesting that this sort of valuation is particularly important, and that it is one that gets overlooked in economic theories of value.[19] If we apply this idea to Moore's perception of the past, we can see that for him the value of the bellows blown pipes is that they afford the opportunity for music making of a kind similar to the traditional music of pre-clearance Scotland. The reinvented music thus represents a Scotland that existed before the influence of competitions and the militarisation of bagpipe music; before the destruction of traditional Scottish culture in colonial Britain. This culture and its music and dance were taken by highlanders to Cape Breton Island, Nova Scotia, in the wave of forced emigration that preceded the full final political absorption of Scotland into the United Kingdom and the dissolution of the old way of life that almost immediately followed. Though it was often brutally hard, consideration of that old way of life and its communal orientation and performance of an oral culture nevertheless presents for many Scots some significant critiques of contemporary Scottish society. By taking his inspiration from such consideration, Moore disengages from an instrumental tradition that absorbed proscription and reflected two hundred years of competition, culture, and the military co-option of the bagpipe. Moore moves his music making, at least to some extent, outside of that discourse. In his performance he offers a discursive disavowal of much of the colonial inspired cultural discourse in Scotland of the last three hundred years.

Yet he is not attempting to revise a musical museum as the preceding paragraph might suggest. Though he plays an older, rhythmic style of Scottish music, he plays it on an instrument that he has built to fit contemporary social space: the pub, the public dining room, the kitchen, the stage, the studio; and in various contexts, many of which were

---

[18] Paul Eiss, "Beyond the Object: Of Rabbits, Rutabagas and History," *Anthropological Theory* 8, no. 1 (2008): 79-97.
[19] Ibid.

unknown prior to contemporary performance: the session, the folk band, the chamber piping ensemble.

> Indeed, the small pipes are not generally found in Cape Breton Music at all. Just as he (and others) did with the small pipes and Scottish music, Hamish Moore is to an extent inventing a tradition.[20]

In building his pipes and playing them, Moore performs his pride in the survival of Scottish emigrants to Nova Scotia after they were driven from their land. He simultaneously rejects many of the cultural changes that took place in Scotland after the 1706–7 Acts of Union, the Jacobite rebellions that followed, and the dissolution of the old social structure. Yet he fits this performance to the contemporary world and thus to an imaginary of the Scotland of today and of the future. His performance of Scottish traditional music in this context is thus a performance of his commitment to Scottish community and oral culture in a contemporary context even as he plays.

And here seems a suitable place to present what has been something of an umbrella idea that has informed my investigation into performance and artisanal instrument making: Jill Dolan's discussions of utopian performance.[21] In these, she,

> investigates the potential of different types of performance to inspire moments in which audiences feel themselves allied with each other, and with a broader, more capacious sense of a public, in which social discourse articulates the possible, rather than the insurmountable obstacles to human potential.[22]

Dolan is speaking about the theatre, arguing that it must present performances that not only criticise the cynicism and political lurch to the right occasioned by the September 11th attacks (for example), but present the possibility of a better future.[23] My contention is that artisanal instrument production and the musical performances that it subsequently facilitates

---

[20] Robin Bynoe, "Review: Review of Hamish Moore – Stepping on the Bridge," Common Stock: The Journal of the Lowland and Borders Pipers' Society 10, no. 2 (1995): 45.

[21] Jill Dolan, "Performance, Utopia, and the 'Utopian Performative,'" Theatre Journal 53, no. 3 (2001): 455-479.; see also Jill Dolan, Utopia in Performance: Finding Hope at the Theatre (Ann Arbor: University of Michigan Press, 2005).

[22] Dolan, *Utopia in Performance*.

[23] Ibid., 3.

represent, in the contemporary neo-liberal Western world, precisely this type of performance. Moore clearly connects "more fully with the complexities of our past and the possibilities of a better future."[24] The inspiring quotation in Dolan's frontispiece is the oft quoted passage from Ian McEwan's *Saturday*. As McEwan is himself the son of a working class Scotsman the passage is worth presenting once more in this context, even if his character is discussing a performance of the blues.

> There are these rare moments when musicians together touch something sweeter than they've ever found before in rehearsals or performance, beyond the merely collaborative or technically proficient, when their expression becomes as easy and graceful as friendship or love. This is when they give us a glimpse of what might be, of our best selves, and of an impossible world in which you give everything you have to others, but lose nothing of yourself. Out in the real world there exist detailed plans, visionary projects for peaceable realms, all conflicts resolved, happiness for everyone, for ever—mirages for which people are prepared to die and kill. Christ's kingdom on earth, the workers' paradise, the ideal Islamic state. But only in music, and only on rare occasions, does the curtain actually lift on this dream of community, and it's tantalisingly conjured, before fading away with the last notes.[25]

Moore's utopia is not one that McEwan mentions by name, but his instruments, and the performances that they facilitate, project the idea of a Scotland based in community and fellowship, and his instruments themselves don't fade away with their last notes, but carry this utopian ideal forward.

Communication

The second of Glassie's three master contexts is communication. He points out that, "in some kinds of performance, creation and communication coincide. The storyteller composes and presents the tale while communicating, transferring the story directly to another whose presence conditions creation."[26] Often, however, they do not. In Glassie's example, he compares a Turkish rug maker, whose rugs are most frequently sold away from her village, with a writer, whose work is read subsequently and at a distance. In the artisanal instrument maker's case, he is somewhere in

---

[24] Ibid., 6.
[25] Ian McEwan, Saturday (London: Jonathan Cape, 2006), 171.
[26] Glassie, 54.

between the storyteller and the rug maker, and might better be likened to a poet whose work may be read later at a distance from its creator, but which might equally well be read by herself, or which might delivered by another reader with the poet in the audience. That is to say, Moore's pipes travel away from him through time and across space, played by other musicians, but he also plays them himself, and other musicians play them in his presence. The instruments carry meaning, congealed intention, history, and the social action and situation of their maker. Most commonly they travel in commerce, but quite frequently they return to his view, often carrying different meanings than those which they carried away.

Take my own set of Moore smallpipes in the key of D, for example, made of African blackwood with boxwood and brass mounts. They were made in 1990 and bought by Neil Anderson, a professional piper who played them on a recording and in a touring band in the United States. Subsequently, they were bought by a college student who owned them for several years, rarely played them, and sold them when he decided that he would prefer to try to learn the uilleann or union pipes. He sold them to a Dr. Jones, an internet dealer of traditional Irish instruments in Idaho, and I traded a flute and two whistles for them in 2007. I have since contacted Moore and his son Fin, and will be returning with the pipes to the workshop in Dunkeld to play them in the company of the Moores while I conduct further research into their pipe-making, twenty-one years after Hamish made them and sent them from his shop. Initially and continually passed on in commerce, the context of these pipes' communication is significantly different to, for example, the set of pipes that the Moores donated to the Pipers' Gathering to be auctioned off as a fundraiser for that organisation. The donated pipes resonated as a gift, communicating not only Moore's skill as a maker publicly and performatively, but the donation was also a performance of his support of piping organizations that promote social and communal piping. My pipes, meanwhile, have reentered the context of communication several times as an item of sale from one consumer to another, each of whom subsequently involved them in different contexts of consumption and further performance.

Consumption

Glassie's final master context is consumption in which "the consumer's reaction overlaps the creator's intentions." As in creation, the artifact exists here in many contexts collecting meanings, some of which may mesh with the intentions of its maker, but many of which will eclipse them.[27] Allow me to once more present the story of my own pipes. For their first owner, the professional musician Neil Anderson, they were the tool of his trade, a workhorse instrument for a working musician: years of gigs in a multiplicity of places and venues, solid and reliable. In this they almost certainly served one of the possible purposes that Moore envisioned for them—that of playing with other instruments in general, and a folk band in particular.

For the young student to whom he sold them, on the other hand, they were an impulsive purchase in an initial enthusiasm for "celtic" music, representing an entry into that collection of traditions and their social places, and were first in a long line of purchases and (relatively) quick sales of various types of bagpipes, whistles and accordions. To the point of our last communication, he has never been able to play any of them with any great competence (though this is by no means to suggest that he never will gain such skill). Moore is painfully aware though, as all the instrument makers that I've spoken to are, that in the elective belonging of liquid modernity, the sale of fine instruments as cultural signifiers without any likely prospect of concomitant musical performance is made necessary by the economic realities of making a living as an instrument maker.[28] Even so, this example of meaning in consumption is clearly quite apart from that of his own intentions or hopes for one of his instruments.

For Dr. Jones, the internet instrument dealer who makes his living as a veterinarian, buying and trading the pipes was an attempt to generate funds for an orphanage in Haiti to which all his profits from instrument sales go. The site also acts as his own musical swap shop, allowing him to try all sorts of interesting instruments before selling most of them on to others, while also connecting those others with instruments that are frequently difficult to find, especially without a wait. In this case (though Moore no doubt recognises the likelihood of his instruments being bought

---

[27] Glassie, 57.

[28] The motivations of those who buy instruments, especially repeatedly, without ever managing to become competent in their use in any musical tradition, is, of course, worth an extensive investigation itself, but is far beyond the scope of this chapter. In the spirit of this inquiry though, I would quickly and simplistically speculate that one possible motivation is that these buyers see the value and meaning expressed in the performance, and are appealed to enough by them to expend economic capital in their pursuit, but either not enough for them to prioritise the labour required to make that performance themselves—or they find themselves unable to expend that labour.

and sold by a dealer for profit) it seems unlikely that he would have considered that his pipes might become a profit generator for a Haitian orphanage. There remains an incongruity between the meanings Moore and Jones attach to the instruments they engage with.

The pipes provide me with an instrument more appropriate to play in the Scottish tradition than my primary one, the Irish flute, which makes an appearance there relatively rarely. Moore's smallpipes grant me a way to engage that tradition and repertoire in a traditional manner, while they satisfy an ambition to play Scottish bagpipes that I have held since my parents took me to watch the pipe bands at the Lord Mayor's Show as a child in Liverpool. I spoke earlier of the instrument maker's projections for the future. When Moore sold his instruments away to America I wonder whether he anticipated their return in the hands of an academic researcher looking into meaning in his work?

The Revival, Consumption and Control

There is, of course, no question of the instrument maker's creative vision holding sway in totality through the process of consumption. In consumption the meanings of the consumer at the very least mediate those of the creator. To return to the revival of the bellows driven pipes, the LBPS' initial initiative with the new instrument attempted to head off a simple wholesale co-option of it by the existing highland tradition. In spite of these concerns, which could be seen, according to Andy Hunter, in an "early policy of discouraging "Highland/pipe band repertoire [which] meant that we were divorcing ourselves from the major piping tradition of Scotland," a survey published in *Common Stock* in 1994 found that 61% of its members characterized themselves as Highland pipers, the majority of whom almost certainly play them in the same manner, if not the same context, that they play their Great Highland Bagpipes.[29] A more recent article in *Common Stock* by David Taylor argued that the situation was even more lopsided than that, and a failure of the Lowland and Border Pipers' Society itself.

---

[29] Hunter, 4; see also Jock Agnew, "Piper's Survey," Common Stock: The Journal of the Lowland and Borders Pipers' Society 9, no. 1 (1994): 22.

We are not in fact the LBPS; we are the HBPS, the Highland Bellows Pipers Society. 99% of all pipers playing bellows pipes are playing highland tunes in highland style.[30]

Clearly, makers, caught between economic realities of production and their own non-economic valuation of the instruments, are unable to keep control of the latter. This is illustrated by the number of fine instruments that are sold to people who, in the view of the maker, will never be able to do them justice. In spite of this lack of control, however, it is also clear that even in the hands of Highland pipers, Moore's ambitions are not swamped entirely and his vision of bagpiping still strongly affects their playing—an artifact, after all, cannot be unlimited in its affordances: it must always facilitate some uses and limit others. Moore's new bagpipes demanded new performance contexts regardless of players' prior experience and intention. Not only did they allow regular playing indoors, they necessitated it, as the smallpipes are not loud enough for any but the quietest and smallest outdoor performance. In only this aspect, in simply changing the place of performance, bellows blown pipes dramatically changed the meaning of the bagpipe by placing bagpipe music once more in social spaces; by bringing pipers once more into the kitchen, into the public house, by placing them comfortably by the hearth.

Nor, to give a further example of their lack of control once the instruments are in the context of consumption, could pipe-makers even direct the physicality and sonority of the instrument. For example, while agreeing on the benefits of standardising the smallpipes, they entirely failed to predict the key (of the instrument's fundamental note) to which production of the smallpipes would gravitate. Writing in the June 1991 edition of *Common Stock,* Collin Ross proposed *D*, arguing that it would sit well with other traditional instruments in sessions. In the following issue, Jock Agnew countered that *C* would be better, and drew up a list of reasons he deemed logical. However, according to a survey of pipe-makers that Agnew himself published in the June 1992 issue, just a year later, pipes in *A* and *D* were being ordered in equal numbers, and by 2000, against all expectation, *A* had become the de facto standard key of the Scottish smallpipe. This was because, rather neatly, it was the key that both pipers and fiddlers thought best matched the fiddle, a combination that has become very popular and, not coincidently, a match that one

---

[30] David Taylor, "The Aspen Tree and the Border Pipe," Common Stock: The Journal of the Lowland and Borders Pipers' Society 29, no. 2 (2012): 16.

imagines ought to have been entirely within the vision of the pipe makers.[31]

However, by contrast there are clear examples of Moore's vision directly influencing performing musicians. One in particular is that of Davie Robertson, who is well known for singing with his pipes and shares Moore's liking of a pre-highland clearances way of making music. He explains the sound he is trying to produce:

> To sum up then, I am trying to sound as I imagine an intelligent eighteenth-century countryman would have sounded, who was not endowed with musical genius, but loved the heritage and tradition, and found it vibrant and meaningful. I suppose the ultimate aim is to sound as if the tradition had lasted into the twentieth-century and up to the present day, and that I was a part of it and had some small contribution of my own to add to it in carrying it on. That is my idea of authenticity, and if I ever manage to touch on it, I will be more than satisfied.

> Being musically illiterate, and never having been taught piping, I am trying to imitate this sound in my head, blissfully free of the shackles of accepted Highland piping technique, and the dictates of the black dots on a printed page.[32]

As his own commentary on it makes clear, Robertson's view of music making is a splendid example of value being signified in performance, as Eiss suggests is so often the case. In this case, his performative valuing just as clearly matches Moore's—music making that partakes of an older tradition not for its own sake, but for the meanings that type of music making carries; the consumer's meaning in this case coinciding with that of the creator. But it would be entirely impossible for Robertson to make this performance without Moore's (or some other pipemaker's) equivalent performance. Singing with the pipes could not be managed were it not for the reinvention of the smallpipes, as they are the only Scottish bagpipe quiet enough to complement the human voice. Moreover, just as important

---

[31] Jock Agnew, "Pipemakers' Survey," Common Stock: The Journal of the Lowland and Borders Pipers' Society 7, no. 1 (1992): 7; see also Hamish Moore "National Museum." Notwithstanding this arrival at A as the standard pitch of the Scottish smallpipes, in my recent interviews with makers there seems to be somewhat of a consensus that while A remains the dominant pitch in terms of orders, there has recently been something of a swing back toward pipes pitched in D.

[32] David Robertson, "Singing to the Sma' Pipes," Common Stock: The Journal of the Lowland and Borders Pipers' Society 8, no. 1 (1993): 17.

in this example is the freeing of the bagpipe from the competition and pipe band tradition's prescription and literacy, a liberation wrought by Hamish Moore and his fellow makers through their development of the new pipes. For Robertson, this performance, which values heritage, tradition and a type of personal music making is, itself, personal. In Moore's case, however, his performance demonstrates not only his own valuing of that kind of music making, it also demonstrates the importance he places on facilitating that sort of tradition for others. As such, in the playing of the pipes while singing, Moore's influence is immediately felt. In fact, it is indispensable.

Conclusion

How much does the artisanal instrument maker partake in a musical performance? I have attempted to address this question by approaching it from three related theoretical directions, all of which see performance as a fundamental way of demonstrating meaning and value. Henry Glassie's performance based approach to material culture involves examining an object in various contexts, particularly those moments of creation, communication and consumption. In each, one can attempt to descry the meaning of the object for those who come into contact with it. Glassie's theory proposes that in the use or consumption of the instrument—in its playing—meanings and intentions of the maker which are carried by the artifact come into contact with a meaning making performance process of the musician. At this point of tension there ensues a negotiation that produces new meanings. The strength of meaning and the affordances carried by an artifact are widely variable, and I hope it is clear that in the case of Scottish bellows bagpipes, the instruments carry their makers' intentions and ideology very strongly, producing significant change in the way music is made by their consumers.

Paul Eiss supplied the second theory, which proposes that one can observe the value placed on an object and an understanding of its history in performative use of the artifact. This idea is exemplified here in one instance by the case of Davie Robertson, who sings while he plays the pipes. He quite clearly states that the value of his music making is in skirting approximately two hundred years of musical history to find an oral tradition relatively free of proscription, and it is equally clear that it is Hamish Moore's instruments and those like them, created out of a similar ideology, that, both practically and conceptually, allow him to do so.

These two theories are knit together by Jill Dolan's discussion of utopian performance—the idea that one can perform the world, or society, or Scotland, that one dreams of, and that this performance can influence others. Moore's instruments are one such performance and Davie Robertson's singing with the pipes another, but it is Moore's pipes that afford Robertson his utopia.

Each of these theories indexes a strong presence of the instrument maker in the moment of a performance during which his instrument is being used, a presence carried by that instrument. This presence is frequently ignored in considerations of performance, as much by musicians, critics and audiences as it is by academics, and it seems to me that more attention might usefully be paid to it in considering the significant change in musicking and meaning it is capable of exerting. As Moore himself points out, in the case of bellows blown Scottish bagpipes, "the whole social context of the instrument has changed, from outdoor performance to the mixed session and folk band."[33] Moore and his fellow pipemakers have entirely transformed the meaning of Scottish bagpiping. In producing new bagpipes fit for contemporary performance contexts that yet hark back to Scottish history and an idea of communal music making. They make instruments that remain iconically Scottish but that facilitate new meanings in performance, performance in which their own views of modern Scottish life resonate strongly.

Works Cited

Agnew, Jock. "Pipemakers' Survey." *Common Stock: The Journal of the Lowland and Borders Pipers' Society* 7, no.1 (1992): 7-11.
—. "Piper's Survey." *Common Stock: The Journal of the Lowland and Borders Pipers' Society* 9, no. 1 (1994): 22-25.
Bynoe, Robin. "Review: Review of Hamish Moore—Stepping on the Bridge." *Common Stock: The Journal of the Lowland and Borders Pipers' Society* 10, no. 2 (1995): 45.
Cheape, Hugh. *Bagpipes: A National Collection of a National Treasure.* Edinburgh: National Museums of Scotland, 2007.
—. "'Happy We've Been a' Thegither': New Directions in Piping." *Common Stock: The Journal of the Lowland and Borders Pipers' Society* 23, no. 2 (2008): 11-16.

---

[33] Fred Freeman, "A Return to Home Ground," Common Stock: The Journal of the Lowland and Borders Pipers' Society 22, no. 2 (2007): 13.

Looking

Dolan, Jill. "Performance, Utopia, and the 'Utopian Performative.'" *Theatre Journal* 53, no. 3 (2001): 455-479.

—. *Utopia In Performance: Finding Hope at the Theatre*. Ann Arbor: University of Michigan Press, 2005.

Eiss, Paul. "Beyond the Object: Of Rabbits, Rutabagas and History." *Anthropological Theory* 8, no.1 (2008): 79-97.

Freeman, Fred. "A Return to Home Ground." *Common Stock: The Journal of the Lowland and Borders Pipers' Society* 22, no. 2 (2007): 4-13.

Gibson, John G. *Traditional Gaelic bagpiping, 1745-1945*. Montreal: McGill-Queen's University Press, 1998.

Glassie, Henry H. *Material Culture*. Bloomington: Indiana University Press, 1999.

Greensitt, Robert. "Letters." *Common Stock: The Journal of the Lowland and Borders Pipers' Society* 7, no.1 (1992): 3.

Hunter, Andy. "Letters." *Common Stock: The Journal of the Lowland and Borders Pipers' Society* 8, no. 2 (1993): 2-5.

Lochridge, Kara M. "'Where Can I Get a Flute Like Yours?:' Art and Material Culture in the Irish Flute Tradition." PhD diss., Indiana University, 2005.

MacInnes, Iain. *The Highland Bagpipe: The Impact of the Highland Societies of London and Scotland, 1781-1844*. Edinburgh: University of Edinburgh Press, 1989.

—. "Taking Stock: Lowland and Border Piping in a Highland World." In *The Highland Bagpipe: Music, History, Tradition*, edited by Joshua Dickson, 169-191. Aldershot: Ashgate, 2009.

McEwan, Ian. *Saturday*. London: Jonathan Cape, 2006.

Moore, Hamish. *Stepping on the Bridge*, Audio CD, Original Edition, Greentrax Records, CDTRAX073, East Lothian, (1994): liner notes, 6.

—. "National Museum of Scotland Craft Exhibition Essay." hamishmoore.com, http://www.hamishmoore.com/essay.htm#intro.

Robertson, Davie. "Singing to the Sma' Pipes." *Common Stock: The Journal of the Lowland and Borders Pipers' Society* 8, no.1 (1993): 17-19.

Schechner, Richard. *Performance Studies: An Introduction*. London: Routledge, 2002.

Seattle, Matt. "Letters." *Common Stock: The Journal of the Lowland and Borders Pipers' Society* 9, no.1 (1994): 4.

Taylor, David. "The Aspen Tree and the Border Pipe." *Common Stock: The Journal of the Lowland and Borders Pipers' Society* 29, no. 2 (2012): 16-23.

CHAPTER FIVE

REMEMBERING THE PAST:
THE MARKETING OF TRADITION
IN NEWFOUNDLAND

PAUL SMITH

Introduction

The goal of this chapter is to explore some of the ways in which "Remembering the Past" has in recent years become the focus of certain sectors of the market economy in Newfoundland, Canada.[1] It is not the intention, therefore, to take an advocational stance and say "this is how to market tradition." Instead, what is offered is an insight into some of the circumstances which appear to have brought about the marketing of traditions in the province, especially Christmas mumming——a multifaceted seasonal tradition with a documented history covering at least two-

[1] The editors are grateful to The Royal Gustavus Adolphus Academy for Swedish Folk Kulture (Kungl. Gustav Adolfs Akademien för Svensk folkkultur) for permission for the author to draw upon his earlier essay "Remembering the Past: The Marketing of Tradition in Newfoundland" from Masks and Mumming in the Nordic Area (Acta Regiae Gustavi Adolphi 98, 2007). They are also grateful to Cambridge Scholars Publishing Ltd for allowing the reprint. The author would like to take this opportunity to thank the following individuals who have contributed in various ways to this chapter. These include: Jeanette Brown, Eddie Cass, Jeff Green of the Downhomer magazine, Martha Griffiths, Anna Guigné, Paul Gruchy, Helen Hartnell, the late Herbert Halpert, Thomas Hutchings, Hanne Pico Larsen, Jodi McDavid, Lara Maynard, Peter Millington, O'Brien's Music Store, Julie Parsons, Gerald Pocius, Michael J. Preston and Gerald Thomas. Last, but not least, a big thanks goes to the members of staff of the Department of Folklore at Memorial University. These include the secretaries, Sharon Cochrane and Cindy Turpin, publications assistant, Eileen Collins, and Patricia Fulton and Pauline Cox of the Memorial University Folklore and Language Archive.

hundred years.[2]

In today's "sophisticated" society, we have little option but to accept that traditions are not simply the prerogative of "the folk," or that they are solely communicated by word-of-mouth, or that there exists a single "natural context" for their practice and/or communication. Instead, everyone, regardless of age, gender, class or race, consciously and/or unconsciously, practices and/or communicates a variety of cultural traditions using the most relevant and accessible means, and in whatever contexts they deem to be appropriate. Similarly, if an alien visiting our world——as we are told they do on a regular basis——were to survey the traditional cultural landscape——which is supposed to be based on continuity and consistency, and to maintain symmetry and pattern——they would find many inconsistencies in that landscape. For example, the *migration* of traditions via communications technology, such as the telephone, the FAX machine and the internet, has meant that the earlier patterns of *diffused* transmission have become distorted. Similarly, the *revival* of traditions, and the heightened awareness as to the *value* of tradition have meant that many traditions have survived little changed long after they have become redundant. It is feasible, therefore, to consider that the marketing of traditions, however undertaken, should join the list of processes which are seen to modify the pattern of the traditional cultural landscape.[3]

Having said that, we also need to recognise that folklorists have both positive and negative views as to the appropriateness of the marketing of tradition. On the one hand, there are those who subscribe to the *Organic Growth Model*, where marketing is seen to be a naturally occurring process. On the other hand, there are those who subscribe to the *Rape and Pillage Model*, where marketing is seen to use and abuse tradition. It is the first of these approaches——the *Organic Growth Model*——to which I subscribe, primarily because I consider that, as a professional folklorist, it is not my job to pass judgement as to the value, merit or appropriateness of a tradition or a related process. Instead, I see my task as being to document

---

[2] Rev. Lewis Amadeus, A History of the Island of Newfoundland (London: The Author, 1819). See also Herbert Halpert and G.M. Story, eds. Christmas Mumming in Newfoundland: Essays in Anthropology, Folklore, and History (Toronto: University of Toronto Press, 1968).

[3] Richard A. Peterson, "Five Constraints on the Production of Culture: Law, Technology, Market, Organizational Structure and Occupational Careers," Journal of Popular Culture 16, no. 2 (1982): 145-146.

and attempt to analyse and interpret what is happening to our traditional culture today.

   The marketing of traditions is not new, and a number of them, customs being a good example,[4] incorporate aspects of self-promotion and marketing by the performers/participants. For instance, the concluding lines of many mummers' plays in Britain ask for remuneration, as in the following example from Sedgefield, County Durham.

> Here comes Johnny Funny
> That comes in to gather the money
> Holes in me pockets, holes in me cap
> But we have an old tin can
> To carry the cash [5]

At the same time, in addition to self-promotion and marketing by the performers/participants, we have also seen the involvement of individuals having specialist external roles, such as mediators, interpreters, brokers and entrepreneurs. For instance, in the seventeenth, eighteenth and nineteenth centuries, numerous printers developed considerable businesses based on producing broadsides with texts drawn from oral tradition, including folk plays.[6] In the twenty-first century, we see artists, writers and media personnel, producers of items of popular culture and events organisers working in a similar way——taking examples of traditions and producing their versions of them for the market place.
   While some mediators, interpreters, brokers and entrepreneurs work

---

[4] J.D.A. Widdowson, "Trends in the Commercialization of English Calendar Customs: A Preliminary Survey," in Aspect of British Calendar Customs, eds. Theresa Buckland and Juliette Wood, 23-35 (Sheffield: Sheffield Academic Press for The Folklore Society, 1993).

[5] Eddie Cass and Steve Roud, An Introduction to the English Mummers' Play (London: English Folk Dance and Song Society/Folklore Society, 2002), 97.

[6] Boyes Georgina, Michael J. Preston and Paul Smith, Chapbooks and Traditional Drama. Part II. Christmas Rhyme Books (Sheffield: National Centre for English for English Cultural Tradition, 1999); Eddie Cass, Michael J. Preston and Paul Smith, "The Peace Egg Book: an Anglo-Irish Chapbook Connection Discovered," Folklore 114, no. 1 (2003): 29-52; Michael J. Preston, M.G. Smith and Paul Smith, "The Peace Egg Chapbook in Scotland: an Analytic Approach to the Study of Chapbooks," The Bibliotheck 8, no. 3 (1976): 71-90; Michael J. Preston, M.G. Smith and Paul Smith, Chapbooks and Traditional Drama. Part I. Alexander and the King of Egypt (Sheffield: Centre for English Cultural Tradition and Language, 1977).

with their own indigenous traditions, others are presenting and promoting traditions with which they perhaps have had little prior experience.[7] More to the point, the goals of those involved in these later-evolving specialist roles are possibly not shared by the performers/participants in the traditions. While the two groups may, for example, share a common goal of obtaining a reward for services rendered, aspects of the social basis of tradition[8] are possibly stronger among indigenous performers/participants than among mediators, interpreters, brokers and entrepreneurs. Furthermore, issues of time and space may separate the two groups. While the performers/participants, at least in theory, tend to uphold the traditional times and places to perform, when we turn to mediators, interpreters, brokers and entrepreneurs, especially when they are marketing artifacts as opposed to performances *per se*, we find that they do not appear to be bound by such concerns. However, we need to acknowledge that it is over-simplistic to consider performers/participants and mediators, interpreters, brokers and entrepreneurs as being two distinct groups. Instead, in numerous instances we see the activities of the two groups overlapping, sometimes a decision being driven by the performers/participants and at other times by the mediators, interpreters, brokers and entrepreneurs.

The common thread underlying the marketing of tradition is a three-step circular decision-making process which embraces:

- *The acquisition of traditions* by prospective mediators, interpreters, brokers and entrepreneurs. Here the role-relationship of the individual to a tradition is determined by decisions made by him/her. The quality/quantity of detail available to them about the tradition is, however, decided by their degree of access to the tradition and/or information about it, and is determined by the *distance* (be it social, physical and/or conceptual) between them and that which they wish to market.

- *The sculpting of traditions* at the hands of prospective mediators, interpreters, brokers and entrepreneurs. In contrast to the performers/participants of a tradition, who in general appear to *replicate* the texts/performance and so on from one year to the next

---

[7] Annie E. Proulx, The Shipping News (New York: Charles Scribner's Sons, 1993), 281; also Stuart Pierson, "Review of Annie E. Proulx, *The Shipping News* (1993)," Newfoundland Studies 11, no. 1 (1995): 151-153.
[8] Georgina Boyes, "The Institutional Basis of Performance: A Socio-Economic Analysis of Contemporary Folk Plays," Roomer 2, no. 6 (1982): 41-44.

with only minor changes occurring, with the mediators, interpreters, brokers and entrepreneurs, we find the more frequent conscious use of *transformation* (the process of modifying an existing tradition) and *simulation* (the process of creating new texts/performances and so on, which appear to be like existing ones). These are not, however, three individual processes, but instead form a continuum of processes which may be applied simultaneously to different aspects of a tradition.

- *The marketing of traditions* by prospective mediators and so on, which coincidentally can provide the basis for the *acquisition of traditions* by others. The manner in which individual traditions are marketed is determined by the perception the prospective mediators, interpreters, brokers and entrepreneurs have of the market/audience for their product, their personal goals, and the way in which the function(s) of those goals are to be fulfilled. The range of possible functions is in this instance wide and, as we shall see, in conjunction with making money for the mediators, interpreters, brokers and entrepreneurs, can range from heightening awareness about political issues, to the provision of entertainment and education, and to remembering the past.

Christmas Mumming in Newfoundland

Christmas mumming in Newfoundland comprises three distinct but related traditions:

- An informal house-visit: a tradition which still exists.

- An informal house-visit with the formal performance of a play: a tradition which has essentially died out, although attempts have been made to revive it.

- A formal outdoor procession:[9] a tradition which has since died out.

Irrespective of which of the three traditions we are considering, certain common elements appear to be present. First, the participants are an informal group of varying composition. Second, the participants attempt a

---

[9] "Our Christmas Number: A Gem of Typographer's Art. Original from Exordium to Peroration," The Evening Telegraph, December 5, 1887, 4.

complete disguise of the face and body, including the use of gender and occupational reversals, gestures and movements, and also the voice, including the use of ingressive speech. Third, the behaviour of the disguised participants tends to be uninhibited. Fourth, the tradition is taken, by the participants, to the audience. Fifth, in the case of the two house-visit traditions, as an issue of reciprocity, the participants have an expectation that they will be rewarded for their activities in some way, the more usual rewards being drink and food.[10] Of the three traditions, it appears to be the "informal house-visit," which has become the primary focus of the current commodification efforts by mediators, interpreters, brokers and entrepreneurs although attention has certainly also been given to the other forms.

The Marketing of Christmas Mumming in Newfoundland

When surveying the range of marketed materials relating to the tradition of Christmas Mumming in Newfoundland, a surprising number of items have been identified, which could variously be categorised as belonging to either popular or elite culture, or falling somewhere between the two.[11] Excluding academic discussions and writings, these include among others:

- *Paintings and Illustrations*. These range from etchings and prints by David Blackwood,[12] oil paintings from Jean Mitchell Cross,

---

[10] Herbert Halpert, "A Typology of Mumming," in Christmas Mumming in Newfoundland: Essays in Anthropology, Folklore, and History, eds. Herbert Halpert and G.M. Story (Toronto: University of Toronto Press, 1969), 36-38.

[11] Regrettably, in the context of this chapter, it has not been possible to present illustrations of all the material documented. Wherever possible, however, references have been given to published works about these items and the artists and others who created them. Details about some of the artists, and examples of their work, are also available through personal web sites and gallery web sites as indicated, and the web site of the Craft Council of Newfoundland and Labrador (Craft Council, http://www.craftcouncil.nf.ca/membership/our-juried-members/). Each of these sites were accessed last on 28th February 2013. In some instances, however, there is no accessible material about the artists and, in a number of instances, they are no longer traceable.

[12] Abbozzo Gallery, http://david-blackwood.abbozzogallery.com (accessed February 28, 2013); David Blackwood, Mummers' Veil: Exhibition Catalogue (Oakville, Ontario: Abbozzo Gallert, 2003); William Gough, "Mummers:" the Art of David Blackwood (Toronto and Montreal: McGraw-Hill Ryerson, 1988); William Gough, David Blackwood Master Printmaker (Vancouver and Toronto: Douglas and

watercolours by John William Hayward,[13] pastels, watercolours, oil paintings and mono-prints from Brenda McClellan,[14] and watercolours by Mary Pratt,[15] to the images by such "folk artists" as Anne Griffiths of Placentia, photographs by Shirley Gallagher, and the pewter work of Raymond Cox.[16]

- *Commercial Prints.* Many examples have been produced by artists including Louise Colbourne Andrews,[17] Sylvia Ficken, Rod Hand, Danielle Loranger,[18] Richard Steele,[19] Joan Blackmore Thistle,[20] Vaughan-Jackson,[21] and Ellen Jean Wareham.[22]

McIntyre, 2001), 85-99 and 163-175; Barbara Wade Rose, "The Rites of Winter: The Magic and Mystery of Newfoundland Mummers," Imperial Oil Review, (1990): 26-30.

[13] "Fools and Mummers," The Monitor: Newfoundland's Catholic Journal, 2000, http://stjohnsarchdiocese.nf.ca/monitor/fools.html; Christopher O'Dea, The Haywards of St. John: John William Hayward (1843-1913) and Thomas Bowden Hayward (1875-1940) (St. John's Memorial Newfoundland: Memorial University of Newfoundland Art Gallery, 1983): inside back cover; Paul O'Neill, A Seaport Legacy: The Story of St. John's Newfoundland (Erin and Ontario: Press Porcepic, 1976), 655.

[14] Brenda McClellan, Any Mummers in the Night? An Exhibition of the Paintings and Prints Portraying the Intriguing Custom of Newfoundland Mumming by Brenda McClellan: Exhibition Catalogue (St. John's Newfoundland: LSPU Gallery, 1991); Nina Patey, "*Any Mummers in the Night* Stirs Memories," The Newfoundland Herald, November 20, 1991, 18-19; James Wade, "Christmas Mummering Tradition Focus on McClellan Tradition," The Sunday Telegram, November 10, 1991, 15.

[15] Ray Guy and Mary West Pratt, "When Jannies Visited: Remembering an Outport Christmas," Canadian Geographic, November-December, 1993, 36-43.

[16] Gloria Hickey, Metal: 5 Views. Lyben Boykov, Ray Cox, Wesley Harris, Mike Massie, and Jim Maunder (St. John's: Craft Council of Newfoundland and Labrador, 2002), 12-13, 22.

[17] Louise Colbourne Andrews, "Any Mummers 'Loved In,'" Downhomer 15, no. 7 (2002): 3.

[18] Danielle Loranger, "Good Times," Downhomer 10, no. 7 (1997): 2.

[19] Butler Framing, http://butlerframing-galery.com/newfoundlandArtists (accessed February 28, 2013).

[20] Craft Council, Studio Guide: A Guide to a Professional Craft and Visual Artists of Newfoundland and Labrador (St. John's Newfoundland: The Craft Council, 2005), 32.

[21] Mark Vaughan-Jackson, "Memories of the Outport: Exhibit Captures Essence of Daily Life in Coastal Newfoundland During 1930's," The Evening Telegram, February 16, 1996, 16.

- *Ceramic Relief Plaques.* So far only one example has been seen, a white on black relief plaque by Terry White of Corner Brook.

- *Sculptures and Figures.* These range from the *papier mâché* work of Janet Peter,[23] carved wooden figures by Kevin Coates,[24] ceramic tableaux by Joan Parsons Woods,[25] various ceramic items, including broaches, ornaments, mugs, and even biscuit-barrels from Thomas Hutchings,[26] ceramic figures from Barb Roberts, cast metal figures from the Heritage Works on Bell Island, wooden figures and tableaux by the self-described "folk artist" Harry Sullivan of Torbay,[27] and detailed bronze figures of Joan Blackmore Thistle.[28]

- *Dressed Dolls.* These include those dressed by Bette Seward and cloths-pegs dolls by Enid Stevenson.

- *Commercial Recordings.* A number of recitations, songs and instrumental pieces related to mummering have been recorded including, among others, Dave Pike and Tim Brown's "Till the Mummers Song is Sung;"[29] Chuck Simms's "Let the Mummers In;"[30] A. Frank Willis's "Mummer's Night in Oshawa;"[31] and Reg

---

[22] Ellen J. Warenham, "Mummers in Brigus," Downhomer 11, no. 7 (1998): 2.

[23] Craft Council of Newfoundland and Labrador, http://craftcouncil.nf.ca/membership/our-juried-members/ (accessed February 28, 2013); Janet Peter, The Disney-fication of a Newfoundland Tradition: The Evolution and Design of a *papier mâché* Mummers (Paper presented at the Challenging Craft International Conference, Aberdeen, September 8-10, 2004).

[24] Craft Council of Newfoundland and Labrador.

[25] Catherine Dempsey, Paul O'Neill and Darlene Warbanski, eds. Newfoundland: A Place Called Home. Special Memories of Joan Persons Woods in Clay Sculpture (St. John's Newfoundland: Historic Parks Association, 1997), 14.

[26] E-mail communication with the author.

[27] Ryan Davis, "Harry Sullivan," The Scope 6, no. 3 (2010): 6.

[28] Craft Council, *Studio Guide*; Vaughan-Jackson;

[29] David Pike and Tim Brown, "Till the Mummers Song is Sung," Old Friends at Christmas (Paradise, Newfoundland: Dave Pike and Tim Brown, Cassette DPTB-196, 1996), Side B.

[30] Chuck Simms, "Let the Mummers in," Chuck's Christmas Casingle (Brampton, Ontario: Downhome Sound DH8901, c.1989), Side A.

[31] Frank A. Willis, "Mummer's Night in Oshawa," Mummers Night in Oshawa: Christmas with A. Frank Willis (Toronto: Newfoundland Records, CD NRCD-1199, 1999), Track 1; Colin MacLean, "A. Frank Willis Passes Away," The Telegram, February 28, 2011.

Watkins's "Mummers Party Jig."[32]

- *Feature Films*. Traditional materials are frequently incorporated into such feature films,[33] as in the case of *Misery Harbour*[34] which was set in Newfoundland[35] and is based on the book by the Danish-born Norwegian novelist Aksel Sandemose, *En Sjømann går i land*[36] In this film Christmas mumming is integral to one violent climactic scene.

- *Documentaries*. One such recent production was *Mummers & Masks: Sex & Death & Pagan Magic*,[37] produced by Peter Blow and Chris Brookes, which includes a segment on Christmas mumming in Newfoundland.[38] The antics of mummers have also been incorporated into documentaries focusing on the work of individual artists such as David Blackwood[39] and even re-presented to a wider audience as part of *The JVC/Smithsonian Folkways Video Anthology of Music and Dance of the Americas*.[40] In both instance, the material used was taken from the National Film Board of Canada's earlier

[32] Reg Watkins, "Mummers Party Jig," Downhomer Presents...Newfoundland Christmas (St. John's Newfoundland: Avondale Music, CD 02 50821, 1999), Track 14.
[33] Mikel J. Koven, "Folklore Studies and Popular Film and Television: A Necessary Critical Survey," Journal of American Folklore 166, (2003): 176-195; Paul Smith, "Contemporary Legend on Film and Television: Some Observations," Contemporary Legend, no. 2 (1999): 137-154.
[34] *Misery Harbour*, feature film, directed by Nils Galup (1999, Red Ochre Productions, Angel Arena, Triangle Art Production).
[35] Espen Haavardsholm, Misery Harbour: Filmen og Bøkene om Espen Arnakke (Oslo: H. Aschehoug & Co., 1999).
[36] Aksel Sandemose, En Sjømann går i land (Oslo: Gyldental, 1931). [A Sailor Goes Ashore].
[37] *Mummers & Masks: Sex & Death & Pagan Magic*, documentary film, produced by Peter Blow and Chris Brookes, (2002, Lindum Films/Battery Included Co-production).
[38] Linda Sue Chambers, "Mummering Around the World: New Documentary Gets to the Heart of a Beloved Tradition," Downhomer 15, no. 7 (2002): 12-15.
[39] *Blackwood*, documentary film (1976, National Film Board of Canada).
[40] *Mummers' House-Visit...1975*, video recording, (1995, Canada and United States: The JVC/Smithsonian Folkways Video Anthology of Music and Dance of the Americas, vol. 1): Extract 1-15, Notes in Book 1: 41-42.

documentary film, *Musicanada*.[41]

- *Television News Reports*. In January 1988 Radio Canada *Nouvelles De L'Atlantique* broadcast a short item on the mummers in Red Brook.[42]

- *Television Light Entertainment*. For example, CBC Television produced the Christmas special, *A Fortune Bay Christmas*,[43] which featured the group Simani.[44]

- *Television Advertising*. Purity Factories Ltd., a local food manufacturing company, has run commercials with images of mummers to support sales of their "Purity Syrup," a non-alcoholic cordial which is often offered to visitors at Christmas time.[45]

- *Books and Book Illustrations*. These range from the inclusion of images in photographic portfolios[46] to works directed at children, like the recent book by the Toronto children's mystery writer, Lucy M. Falcone, *The Mysterious Mummer*.[47] Likewise, Dawn Baker included a picture of mummers to illustrate the letter "M" in *A Newfoundland Alphabet*.[48]

---

[41] *Musicanada*, documentary film, produced by Tom Daly (1975, National Film board of Canada).
[42] Radio Canada Nouvelles De L'Atlantique, "Mummers in Red Brook Newfoundland," Broadcast January 6, 1988.
[43] CBC Television, "A Fortune Bay Christmas [AKA 'The Mummers Show']," in Here and Now (St. John's: CBC Television, first broadcast January 6, 1986).
[44] "The Mummers Show...," The Newfoundland Herald, December 24, 1994, 21; Gerald L. Pocius, "The Mummers Song in Newfoundland: Intellectuals, Revivalists and Cultural Nativism," Newfoundland Studies 4, no. 1 (1988): 74-75.
[45] Purity Syrup Presents "A Christmas Visit," advertisement (CBC Television, December 1990a,). This is a parody of Simani's "Any Mummers Allowed in?" Segment from CBC Television, "A Fortune Bay Christmas," 1986.
[46] Yva Momatiuk and John Eastcott, This Marvelous Terrible Place: Images of Newfoundland and Labrador (Camden East: Camden House, 1988), 97 and 137.
[47] Lucy M. Falcone, The Mysterious Mummer (Toronto: Kids Can Press, 2003).
[48] Dawn Baker, A Newfoundland Alphabet (Gander, Newfoundland: Art Work Studio, 1998).

- *Short Stories*. These include, among others, "The Mysterious Mummer" by the Newfoundland writer Bert Batstone,[49] and "Will Ye Let the Mummers In?" by the Nova Scotia born writer, the late Alden Nowlan.[50]

- *Poetry*. Numerous pieces on the topic of mumming have appeared over the years, including Rose Sullivan's "Mummering at Christmas"[51] and Eleanor Conway's "Mummering."[52]

- *Newspaper and Magazine Articles*. Perhaps not surprisingly, countless articles have appeared over the years (see, for example, Andrews;[53] Guy and Pratt;[54] Harrington;[55] Mowat;[56] and Rose.[57])

- *Newspaper and Magazine Illustrations*. As early as 1887 the *Christmas Number*.... of the local *Evening Telegram* reproduced a picture of "Water Street, St. John's, N.F. Thirty Years Ago. Mumming Scene and 'Haul of Wood'"[58] an illustration possibly based on one of John William Hayward's pictures.[59] More recently, a detailed set of photographs of mummers accompanied an article by Farley Mowat.[60]

---

[49] Bert Batstone, "The Mysterious Mummer," in The Mysterious Mummer and Other Newfoundland Stories, 110-120 (St. John's Newfoundland: Jesperson Press, 1984).

[50] Alden Nowlan, "Will Ye Let the Mummers in?" in Will Ye Let the Mummers in? Stories by Alden Nowlan, 60-75 (Toronto: Irwin Publishing, 1984).

[51] Rose M. Sullivan, "Mummering at Christmas," The Atlantic Guardian, December 1948, 12.

[52] Eleanor Conway, "Mummering," Downhomer 14, no. 7 (2001): 95.

[53] Andrews op. cit.

[54] Guy and Pratt, op.cit.

[55] Michael Harrington, "Christmas Mummering Revisited," The Evening Telegram, March 5, 1994, 62.

[56] Farley Mowat, "Will Ye Let the Mummers in?" The Evening Telegram Weekend Magazine 16, no. 52 (1966): 6-9.

[57] Rose, op. cit.

[58] "Water Street, St. John's, N.F. Thirty Years Ago. Mumming Scene and 'Haul of Wood,'" Christmas Number, Evening Telegram 5, Christmas 1987.

[59] Harrington, op.cit.

[60] Mowat, op. cit.

- *Magazine Puzzles*. Mel D'Souza,[61] as part of his series of "Spot the Difference" puzzles for the *Downhomer* magazine, produced "Mummering with Ern and Coal Bin." For the same publication Ron Young created "The Newfoundland Logic Problems...."[62]

- *Newspaper and Magazine Advertising*. In its Christmas advertising for "Purity Syrup," the makers have used illustrations of mummers with the caption, "Stock Up Now. You Never Know Who's Going to Drop By."[63] The *Downhomer* magazine has similarly used images of mummers as part of its advertising layouts to attract subscriptions.[64] Conversely, the Newfoundland Liquor Corporation's magazine, *Enjoy*, which is available free at all liquor stores in the province, gave the following mixer recipe for "Mummers Morning" to promote its products; 1 oz. white rum, vodka or gin, Pink Grapefruit juice, Rim glass with sugar.[65]

- *Product Advertising*. Using traditions in this manner is not an altogether new phenomenon,[66] and in this case is best exemplified by the Quidi Vidi Brewing Company which each Christmas produces a beer called "Mummers Brew," the bottle labels having a picture of mummers.[67]

- *Events*. These take various forms, but are usually organised by particular institutions. For example, in 1979 the Corner Brook Arts and Culture Centre hosted the Humber-Bay of Islands Museum

---

[61] Mel D'Souza, "Different Stroke...Mummering with Ern and Coal Bin," Downhomer 4, no. 7 (1991): 25.

[62] Ron Young, "The Newfoundland Logic Problem...The Mummers," Downhomer 11, no. 7 (1998): 47; and Ron Young, "The Newfoundland Logic Problem...Five Mummers," Downhomer 16, no. 7 (2003): 141.

[63] Purity Syrup, "Stock Up Now. You Never Know Who's Going to Drop By," The Evening Telegram, December 1996b, 7. [Advertisement].

[64] "Give them Mummers for Christmas..." Downhomer 7, no. 4 (1994): 56. [Advertisement].

[65] Newfoundland Liquor Corporation, "Holiday Mixer," Enjoy: Newfoundland Liquor Corporation, Holiday issue (2003): 25.

[66] Paul Mercer and Mac Swackhammer, "'The Singing of Old Newfoundland Ballads and a Cool Glass of Good Bear Go Hand in Hand:' Folklore and 'Tradition' in Newfoundland Advertising," Culture and Tradition 3, (1978): 36-45.

[67] Quidi Vidi Brewing Company, http://www.nlbeerhistory.com/category/quidi-vidi-brewing/ (accessed February 28, 2013).

Society's Christmas mummering exhibit.[68] Likewise "Christmas at the Museum" was staged by the Provincial Museum of Newfoundland and Labrador and included a "... Lecture on the mummer tradition by Dr. Martin Lovelace of MUN Folklore Department...;" the "... performance of the *Mummers Play* featuring the Jackie Lantern Players...;" a workshop on how to make a Hobby Horse; and an exhibit called "Mummers at Our Door."[69] In the same year, St. John's Folk Arts Council presented a workshop on "The Mummers Play" as part of a series of similar events on Newfoundland Traditions.[70]

- *"Mummers For Hire."* A number of local performers of one sort and another offer their services as mummers through the local newspapers. Kelly Russell advertised his services as a "Fiddler for Hire. Christmas Parties—Also Mummers Play. Fiddle Lessons...."[71] while Jim Payne offered "Mummers. For your home Christmas party including mummers play, carols and music... Reasonable rates..."[72]

- *Clothing.* Twackwear produced a shirt with the definition "mummer /'mʌmə'/n visitor in disguise at Christmas time" across the chest, and the Downhomer store has produced one with a coloured embroidered picture of three characters in disguise above the logo "Newfoundland Mummers." The same logo was subsequently used by them on tote bags (see below). The *Downhomer* magazine has also marketed "Newfoundland Mummers Fleece Pullovers."[73]

---

[68] "Mummers Material on Display: Christmas Jannies Crash Exhibit Opening," The Western Star, December 10, 1979, 9.

[69] Christmas at the Museum...9th December (St. John's Newfoundland: The Provincial Museum of Newfoundland and Labrador, 2001). [Poster for Christmas events].

[70] St. John's Folk Arts Council, "The Mummers Play: A Workshop by Chris Brookes and Christina Smith," (The Masonic Temple, Cathedral Street, St. John's Newfoundland, November 17, 2001), e-mail notice November 5, 2001.

[71] Kelly Russell, "Fiddler for Hire..." The Evening Telegram, December 13, 1997, 9.

[72] Jim Payne, "Mummers..." The Evening Telegram, December 10, 1991, 12.

[73] "Downhomer Mail Order...Newfoundland Mummers Fleece Pullovers," Downhomer 12, no. 7 (1999): 141.

- *Tote Bags and "Wine Bags."* These have been produced for the Downhomer store and have coloured embroidered pictures of three characters wearing typical mumming disguises, and a logo proclaiming "Mummering Newfoundland."[74]

- *Greeting Cards, Postcards and Note Cards.* Some of these items employ specially designed illustrations, such as Linda Coles's "Christmas Mummers;" Patrick Mackey's "Mummers Down the Lane;" and the untitled cards illustrated by Jim Oldford for Old Harry Rock Creations, and "H" for Outport Designs in Carbonear. The latter, while presenting a contemporary image of Christmas mummers, incorporates lines from P.J. Dyer's nostalgic poem "Terra Novean Exile's Song."[75] Original photographs are also used in some (see, for instance, Rhonda Hayward's "Mummering in Newfoundland"), while others are based on existing original paintings among other things. For example, the series of cards by Brenda McClellan used some of her pictures of mummers, as did Danielle Loranger's "Expected Visitors" and "Secret Dance," Ellen Jean Wareham's "Mummers in Rose Blanche" and "The Mummers," being a photograph of the ceramic tableaux by Joan Parsons Woods.

- *Christmas Tree Ornaments.* Here we have the stencilled glass balls by Alderbrook Industries Ltd. of Pickering, Ontario, Canada[76] and the *papier mâché* ornaments of Janet Peter.[77]

- *Gift Wrapping Paper.* For the past few years GKE Futures has produced Christmas paper with illustrations of mummers.

This list of marketed items relating to Christmas mumming in Newfoundland is lengthy. While it demonstrates the volume and variety of the items on offer, it also shows that the majority of the representations (be they pictures, stories, songs or anything else) depict costumed and disguised mummers in the setting of the informal house-visit. At the same

---

[74] "shopDownhomer.com," *Downhomer* 15, no. 7 (2000): 129.

[75] P.J. Dyer, "Terra Novean Exile's Song," in *Songs and Ballads of Newfoundland, Ancient and Modern,* comp. James Murphy, 36-38 (St. John's Newfoundland: James Murphy, 1902).

[76] Alderbrook Industries Ltd, Pickering Ontario, Canada, c2000.

[77] Craft Council of Newfoundland and Labrador; Peter op. cit.

time, the list also demonstrates the range of qualities and prices that are available: from items in newspapers and $3 greeting cards, to the prints of David Blackwood (c. $2,000 upwards) and the bronze sculptures of Joan Blackmore Thistle (c. $6,500). As we shall see, it is also significant that the majority of these items have been produced in the last ten to fifteen years.

Interpreting the Marketing of Christmas Mumming in Newfoundland

Given this perhaps surprising range of items, we need to consider just what brought about this exceptional focus on one particular seasonal tradition. Gerald Pocius, in his essay "The Mummers Song in Newfoundland: Intellectuals, Revivalists and Cultural Nativism,"[78] argued that the revitalisation among the general population of Newfoundland of the Christmas mumming tradition was the result of a range of cultural activities in the province. This present chapter argues that the current increase in the marketing of representations of Christmas mumming in Newfoundland has occurred as a result of the same range of cultural activities, along with a worsening economic climate.

First, the rise of the nativism movement in the province has meant that certain sectors of the population have become interested in reviving or perpetuating aspects of the local culture, which they perceived as being distinct.[79] This is perhaps not surprising in a place with a high percentage of artists and performers, where we find many local singers performing within the context of the home and local bars; where there are venues to learn traditional local dances; where local companies offer "Legend Tours" by coach; and where participating in traditional/"folk" activities or studying folklore at university is not viewed as weird, but is seen as part and parcel of everyday life. As a consequence, for those insiders and outsiders with a heightened awareness as to the value of traditional culture, in Newfoundland they must think that they have found paradise. Second, the notion of Christmas mumming being perceived as a distinct feature of the local culture stems in part from research undertaken in the 1960s by both the Institute of Social and Economic Research and the Department of Folklore at Memorial University of Newfoundland.[80] This

---

[78] Pocius, op. cit.
[79] Ibid., 58-59.
[80] Ibid., 59-61.

research culminated with the publication in 1969 of *Christmas Mumming in Newfoundland: Essays in Anthropology, Folklore, and History*, edited by Herbert Halpert and George Story. While the book makes no claim for the uniqueness of the tradition, it did highlight it, and so awakened the interest of a new generation in the topics. Third, the revival in the province in the early 1970's of the mummers' play tradition by the highly visible and politically vocal *Mummers Troupe*[81] again awakened interest in Christmas mumming traditions, even if realistically the play tradition was already dead.[82]

Fourth, high levels of unemployment, as much as 80% in some outports, have fostered over the past decades a strong entrepreneurial spirit among the population. This has tended to come to the fore in times of economic downturns, and often the basis for a small new business was a perception that there was a potential market for certain items of traditional culture which reflected distinctiveness. Consequently, many local products, ranging from traditional knitwear to food items, have been the focus of new business ventures. In that respect, the marketing of Christmas mumming is no different and, as a consequence, many of the items and events being marketed have been produced by local individuals, some being performers/participants in the tradition as well as mediators, interpreters, brokers and entrepreneurs. Fifth, given that background, it is perhaps not coincidental that over the past decade numerous "craft shops" have opened across the island and there has been a marked increase in the number of "craft fairs" being promoted. Furthermore, the city of St. John's appears to have almost as many art galleries as bars, all in their own way providing venues for the potential marketing of traditions. Sixth, the high level of unemployment over the years has also meant that since the 1950's, the province has been experiencing an out-migration of its population. The outcome of this has been that as much as 50% of the population born within Newfoundland is, at any one time, absent from the province, often without choice, and desperately wishing to return home.[83] Such "yearnings" fuel nostalgia, not only for the "place" but also for the "period" when they left the island. This results in the opportunity to market products to satisfy that nostalgia. Having said that, the potential

---

[81] Chris Brookes, A Public Nuisance: A History of the Mummers Troupe (St. John's: Institute of Social and Economic Research, Memorial University, 1988).
[82] Pocius, 61-64.
[83] James Overton, Making a World of Difference: Essays on Tourism, Culture and Development in Newfoundland (St. John's: Institute of Social and Economic Research, Memorial University, 1996), 125.

market for such heritage items is complex and includes:
  - Indigenous Newfoundlanders
  - Visiting expatriate Newfoundlanders
  - Expatriate Newfoundlanders purchasing by mail-order
  - External visitors

As James Overton has observed:

> The sellers of various products have sought to identify their commodities with Newfoundland. For Newfoundlanders the product which effectively identifies with Newfoundland encourages the consumer to (re)signify membership of the imagined community by the act of consuming. The symbolic value of the commodity is that it stands as a national-cultural marker. For the non-Newfoundlander consumption of the commodity represents a kind of symbolic visit to the exclusive territory of Newfoundland as a distinctive cultural species.[84]

Seventh, another major contributory factor, itself being an example of the marketing of Christmas mumming, occurred in late November 1983 when the local group Simani,[85] comprising Bud Davidge and Sim Savory from Fortune Bay on the south coast, released a 45 rpm record of the song "Any Mummers Allowed in?"[86] Now known locally as "The Mummer's Song," it describes Christmas mumming in a typical Newfoundland outport home. While this has not been the only song to portray the activities of mummers,[87] it has certainly proved to be the most popular (in the first month after its release it sold 5,500 copies), far surpassing the group's expectations.[88] As a spin off, Bud Davidge of Simani, with Ian Wallace as illustrator, produced *The Mummer's Song*,[89] a children's book based on the song, which could also be bought packaged with an accompanying

---

[84] Ibid., 151.
[85] Geoff Meeker, "Simani: Working Towards a Home-Grown Recording Industry," The Newfoundland Signal 9-15, September 1990, 3-11.
[86] Bud Davidge, A Songbook of Original Newfoundland Songs Written by...as recorded by Simani, vol. 1 (English Harbour West, Newfoundland: SWC Productions, 1997), 4 and 24-27; Simani [Bud Davidge and Sim Savory], "Any Mummers Allowed In?" 45 rpm record (1983, Bel Air: BA 202), Side A.
[87] Dave Pike and Tim Brown, "Till the Mummers Song is Sung," Old Friends at Christmas (Paradise, Newfoundland: cassette DPTB-196, 1996): Side B; Simms op. cit.; Willis op. cit.
[88] Pocius, 64-74.
[89] Bud Davidge and Ian Wallace, The Mummers Song (Toronto and Vancouver: Douglas and McIntyre, 1993).

cassette tape, and subsequently a CD. The continuing popularity of the
song is possibly reflected not only by the fact that it appears in published
song collections,[90] but also that parodies have appeared.[91] As late as 1997
handwritten copies of the verses were being faxed around the province.[92]
Even today copies proliferate on the web, often under the title of "The
Mummer's Song," instead of its original title. At a different level, cover
versions have been performed by a number of performers, including what
is probably at this time the most popular local group, Great Big Sea.[93]
Overall, and most importantly, Simani's "Any Mummers Allowed in?"
has had a direct impact on people's perceptions of mumming and, without
intending to, promoted a revival of the tradition. Perhaps surprisingly, the
song has also become a rallying anthem in the province, a symbol of
cultural identity, and possibly unity.[94] Eighth, CBC Television
subsequently produced a Christmas special, *A Fortune Bay Christmas*,[95]
which was based around the songs of Simani, and which included a
dramatised version of "Any Mummers Allowed in?" Referred to locally as
"The Mummers Show," the programme, with its strong visual images,
became extremely popular. It was re-shown every Christmas for a number
of years, and is still periodically broadcast—so offering a continuing
visual reinforcement as to what the Christmas mumming tradition
supposedly entails.[96] It is probably indicative of the popularity of both the
song and the television programme that Purity Factories Ltd. ran a
television commercial for its "Purity Syrup"[97] which was based on a
dramatisation of "Any Mummers Allowed in?" as it appeared in CBC

---

[90] Eric West, Comfort and Joy: Christmas Songs of Newfoundland and Labrador, vol. 4 (Ladle Cove, Newfoundland: Vinland Music, 2002), 26-27.
[91] Judith Dwyer, "Photocopylore," (Undergraduate Student paper, Folklore 3450: Language and Play, Department of Folklore, Memorial University of Newfoundland, 1991), 79-80.
[92] A handwritten fax with the title "Simani. [Bud Davidge and Sim Savory], "The Mummer's Song" (AKA "Any Mummers Allowed In?")," and dated "18th December 1997," was found by the author in a secondhand copy of Herbert Halpert and G.M. Story. eds. *Christmas Mumming in Newfoundland* in Corner Brook, Newfoundland, in 2003.
[93] Great Big Sea, http://www.youtube.com/watch?v=rpsek6GjcRg, (accessed February 28, 2013).
[94] Pocius, 64-74.
[95] CBC Television, "A Fortune Bay Christmas."
[96] "The Mummers Show." See also Pocius, 74-75.
[97] *Purity Syrup Presents.*

Television's *A Fortune Bay Christmas.*[98]

So what for the future? A Christmas mumming theme park? Perhaps not. But why restrict Christmas mumming to Christmas? It is becoming increasingly popular in the province for mummers to appear as part of family summer festivities for visiting expatriates.[99] Such celebrations are also sometimes organised within the community. As Mel D'Souza writes:

> Our Christmases in Canada have followed the traditional North American Pattern until 1999, when I had my first experience of "Christmas in July" in Ramea, Newfoundland. The community had a Santa Claus, mummers, a turkey dinner and all the trimmings that go with Christmas. This was not only an enjoyable event for me, but it gave people returning to Ramea for a summer holiday the opportunity to celebrate Christmas with family——a get-together that would otherwise not be possible on Christmas Day.[100]

A folklore graduate student travelling on the ferry from Newfoundland to mainland Canada in July 2001 reported the following incident.

> I was witness to a somewhat bizarre, unseasonal mumming scene this past July aboard the Argentia [Newfoundland]——North Sydney [Nova Scotia] ferry during "house" band Nord Easter's performance. About halfway across the Gulf the duo paused from their regular assortment of drum machine-enhanced covers, and broke into a clamorous rendition of "The Mummers Song." Enthusiastic Marine Atlantic staff poured into the air-conditioned lounge from all entrances, dressed in mummers garb and started dancing, singing, etc. with eager tourists. Immediately following the song all the staff promptly exited, people returned to their seats, and the Nord Easter resumed to the standard covers. Ahh, the strange sights and sounds of summer....[101]

Apparently, this is not an isolated incident. The Salmonier Country Manor, an inn situated in Mount Carmel, St. Mary's Bay, about an hour drive out of St John's, offers in its literature a variety of facilities and activities including:

> "Christmas and the Mummers"——an old-fashioned Christmas Dinner and a "Time." Just a wonderful evening of food, music, song, dance, laughter, and of course, a visit from those mysterious "Mummers!" Come Share our

---

[98] "A Fortune Bay Christmas."
[99] Ella Watkins and Ken Watkins, "Snapshots & Stories. Mummers in June," Downhomer 16, no. 7 (2003): 123.
[100] Mel D'Souza, "The Spirit of Christmas," Downhomer 16, no. 7 (2003): 132-133.
[101] Paul Gruchy, E-mail communication, October 3, 2001.

Culture! *Performances held Wednesday evenings throughout June, July, and August (reservations required).*[102]

These performances of "Summer mummering" at the Salmonier Country Manor have also featured on CBC Television's "Here & Now" programme.[103]

Surveys of the students at Memorial University in Newfoundland indicate a current decline of participation in Christmas mumming house-visits. Having said that, the overall interest in the phenomenon of Christmas mumming in Newfoundland is exemplified by the numerous web sites presently devoted to the topic (see, for example, the links listed through the English Folk Play Research Home Page).[104] Furthermore, there is no doubt as to the popularity of the numerous representations of mummers being sold each year, especially, though by no means exclusively, at Christmas time. Taken together, this indicates that perhaps what is actually being marketed, probably more so for the indigenous and expatriate Newfoundlanders than for visitors, has less to do with the tradition of Christmas mumming, than it has to do with remembering the past: nostalgia for a time now gone.

Works Cited

Abbozzo Gallery, http://david-blackwood.abbozzogallery.com.
Alberbrook Industries Ltd, Pickering Ontario, Canada. c.2000.
Andrews, Louise Colbourne. "Any Mummers 'Lowed In." *Downhomer* 15. no. 7 (2002): 3.
Anspach, Rev. Lewis Amadeus. *A History of the Island of Newfoundland.* London: The Author, 1819.
Baker, Dawn. *A Newfoundland Alphabet.* Gander, Newfoundland: Art Work Studio, 1998.
Batstone, Bert. "The Mysterious Mummer." In *The Mysterious Mummer and Other Newfoundland Stories*, 110-120. St. John's, Newfoundland: Jesperson Press, 1984.
Blackwood, Documentary film. National Film Board of Canada, 1976.
Blackwood, David. *The Mummer's Veil: Exhibition Catalogue.* Oakville, Ontario: Abbozzo Gallery, 2003.

---

[102] Emphasis added.
[103] CBC Television, "Summer Mummering at Salmonier Country Manor, Mount Carmel, St. Mary's Bay," in Here and Now, reporter Deborah Collins (St. John's: CBC Television, broadcast July 29, 1999).
[104] http://folkplay.info (accessed February 28, 2013).

Boyes, Georgina. "The Institutional Basis of Performance: A Socio-Economic Analysis of Contemporary Folk Plays." *Roomer....* 2, no. 6 (1982): 41-44.

Boyes, Georgina, Michael J. Preston, and Paul Smith. *Chapbooks and Traditional Drama. Part II. Christmas Rhyme Books.* Sheffield: National Centre for English Cultural Tradition, 1999.

Brookes, Chris. *A Public Nuisance: a History of the Mummers Troupe.* St. John's: Institute of Social and Economic Research, Memorial University, 1988.

Butler Framing, http://butlerframing-gallery.com/newfoundlandArtists.

Cass, Eddie, Michael J. Preston, and Paul Smith. "The Peace Egg Book: An Anglo-Irish Chapbook Connection Discovered." *Folklore* 114, no. 1 (2003): 29-52.

Cass, Eddie and Steve Roud. *An Introduction to the English Mummers' Play.* London: English Folk Dance and Song Society/Folklore Society, 2002.

CBC Television. "A Fortune Bay Christmas [AKA 'The Mummers Show']," In *Here and Now.* St. John's: CBC Television, First broadcast January 6, 1986.

—. "Summer Mummering at Salmonier Country Manor, Mount Carmel, St. Mary's Bay," In *Here and Now*, Reporter Deborah Collins. St. John's: CBC Television, Broadcast July 29, 1999.

Chambers, Linda Sue. "Mummering Around the World: New Documentary Gets to the Heart of a Beloved Tradition." *Downhomer* 15, no. 7 (2002): 12-15.

Christmas at the Museum.... 9th December. St. John's, Newfoundland: The Provincial Museum of Newfoundland and Labrador, 2001. [Poster for Christmas events].

Conway, Eleanor. "Mummering." *Downhomer* 14, no. 7 (2001): 95.

Craft Council. *Studio Guide: A Guide to the Professional Craft and Visual Artists of Newfoundland and Labrador.* St. John's, Newfoundland: The Craft Council, 2005.

Craft Council of Newfoundland and Labrador. (http://www.craftcouncil.nf.ca/membership/our-juried-members/).

Davidge, Bud. *A Songbook of Original Newfoundland Songs Written by... as Recorded by Simani*, vol. 1. English Harbour West, Newfoundland: SWC Productions, 1997.

Davidge, Bud and Ian Wallace. *The Mummer's Song.* Toronto/ Vancouver: Douglas and McIntyre, 1993.

Davis, Ryan. "Harry Sullivan." *The Scope* 6, no. 3 (2010): 6.

Dempsey, Catherine, Paul O'Neill and Darlene Warbanski. eds.

Newfoundland: A Place Called Home. Special Memories of Joan Parsons Woods in Clay Sculpture. St. John's: Newfoundland Historic Parks Association, 1997.

"Downhomer Mail Order.... Newfoundland Mummers Fleece Pullovers." *Downhomer* 12, no. 7 (1999): 141.

D'Souza, Mel. "Different Strokes.... Mummering with Ern and Coal Bin." *Downhomer* 4, no. 7 (1991): 25.

—. "The Spirit of Christmas." *Downhomer* 16. no. 7 (2003): 132-133.

Dwyer, Judith. "Photocopylore." Undergraduate Student Paper, Folklore 3450: Language and Play. Department of Folklore, Memorial University of Newfoundland, 1991. 79-80.

Dyer, P.J. "Terra Novean Exile's Song." In *Songs and Ballads of Newfoundland, Ancient and Modern*, comp. by James Murphy, 36-38. St. John's, Newfoundland: James Murphy, 1902.

English Folk Play Research Home Page, http:/www.folkplay.info.

Falcone, Lucy M. *The Mysterious Mummer*. Toronto: Kids Can Press, 2003.

"Fools and Mummers." *The Monitor: Newfoundland's Catholic Journal..*(2000). http://www.stjohnsarchdiocese.nf.ca/monitor/fools.htm.

"Give them Mummers for Christmas...." *Downhomer* 7, no. 4 (1994): 56. [Advertisement].

Gough, William. *"Mummers." The Art of David Blackwood*. Toronto and Montreal: McGraw-Hill Ryerson, 1988.

—. *David Blackwood Master Printmaker*. Vancouver and Toronto: Douglas and McIntyre, 2001.

Great Big Sea. http://www.youtube.com/watch?v=rpsek6GjcRg.

Greetings From Newfoundland Ltd. http://greetings.webworksinc.com.

Gruchy, Paul. E-mail communication, October 3, 2001.

Guy, Ray and Mary West Pratt. "When Jannies Visited: Remembering an Outport Christmas." *Canadian Geographic* (November-December 1993): 36-43.

Haavardsholm, Espen. *Misery Harbour: Filmen og Bøkene om Espen Arnakke*. Oslo: H. Aschehoug & Co., 1999.

Halpert, Herbert. "A Typology of Mumming." In *Christmas Mumming in Newfoundland: Essays in Anthropology, Folklore, and History*, edited by Herbert Halpert and G.M Storey, 34-61. Toronto: University of Toronto Press, 1969.

Halpert, Herbert and G.M. Story. eds. *Christmas Mumming in Newfoundland: Essays in Anthropology, Folklore, and History*. Toronto: University of Toronto Press, 1969.

Harrington, Michael. "Christmas Mummering Revisited." *The Evening Telegram*, March 5, 1994.

Hickey, Gloria. *Metal: 5 Views. Luben Boykov, Ray Cox, Wesley Harris, Mike Massie and Jim Maunder*. St. John's: Craft Council of Newfoundland and Labrador, 2002.

Koven, Mikel J. "Folklore Studies and Popular Film and Television: A Necessary Critical Survey." *Journal of American Folklore* 116, (2003): 176-195.

Loranger, Danielle. "Good Times." *Downhomer* 10, no. 7 (1997): front cover and 2.

MacLean, Colin. "A. Frank Willis Passes Away." *The Telegram*, February 28, 2011.

McClellan, Brenda. *Any Mummers in the Night? An Exhibition of the Paintings and Prints Portraying the Intriguing Custom of Newfoundland Mummering by Brenda McClellan*. St. John's, Newfoundland: LSPU Gallery, 1991. [Exhibition Catalogue].

Meeker, Geoff. "Simani: Working Towards a Home-Grown Recording Industry." *The Newfoundland Signal* 9-15, (1990): 3, 11.

Mercer, Paul and Mac Swackhammer. "'The Singing of Old Newfoundland Ballads and a Cool Glass of Good Beer Go Hand in Hand': Folklore and 'Tradition' in Newfoundland Advertising." *Culture and Tradition* 3, (1978): 36-45.

Misery Harbour, Feature Film, Directed by Nils Galup. 1999. Red Ochre Productions, Angel Arena, Triangle Art Production.

Momatiuk, Yva and John Eastcott. *This Marvellous Terrible Place: Images of Newfoundland and Labrador*. Camden East: Camden House, 1988.

Mowat, Farley. "Will Ye Let the Mummers In?...." *The Evening Telegram Weekend Magazine* 16, no. 52 (1966): 6-9.

"Mummering Material on Display. Christmas Jannies Crash Exhibit Opening." *The Western Star*, December 10, 1979.

Mummers' House-Visit.... 1975, Video recording. 1995. Canada and the United States: The JVC/Smithsonian Folkways Video Anthology of Music and Dance of the Americas, vol. 1.

Mummers & Masks: Sex & Death & Pagan Magic, Documentary film, Produced by Peter Blow and Chris Brookes. 2002. Lindum Films/Battery Included Co-production.

"The Mummers Show...." *The Newfoundland Herald*, December 24, 1994.

Musicanada, Documentary film, Produced by Tom Daly. 1975. National Film Board of Canada.

Newfoundland Liquor Corporation. "Holiday Mixer." *Enjoy: Newfoundland*

Liquor Corporation, Holiday Issue (2003): 25.

Nowlan, Alden. "Will Ye Let the Mummers In? In *Will Ye Let The Mummers In? Stories by Alden Nowlan*, 60-75. Toronto: Irwin Publishing, 1984.

O'Dea, Christopher. *The Haywards of St. John's: John William Hayward (1843-1913) and Thomas Bowden Hayward (1875-1940)*. St. John's, Newfoundland: Memorial University of Newfoundland Art Gallery, 1983.

O'Neill, Paul. *A Seaport Legacy: The Story of St. John's, Newfoundland.* Erin, Ontario: Press Porcepic, 1976.

"Our Christmas Number. A Gem of the Typographer's Art. Original from Exordium to Peroration." *The Evening Telegram*, December 5, 1887.

Overton, James. *Making a World of Difference: Essays on Tourism, Culture and Development in Newfoundland.* St. John's: Institute of Social and Economic Research, Memorial University, 1996.

Patey, Nina. "*Any Mummers in the Night* Stirs Memories." *The Newfoundland Herald*, November 20, 1991.

Payne, Jim. "Mummers...." *The Evening Telegram*, December 10, 1991.

Peter, Janet. "The Disney-fication of a Newfoundland Tradition: The Evolution and Design of *Papier Mâché* Mummers." Paper presented at the Challenging Craft International Conference, Gray's School of Art, Aberdeen, September 8-10, 2004. http://www2.rgu.afc.uk/Challengingcraft/ChallengingCraft/indexofpapers/identitylocalglobal.htm.

Peterson, Richard A. "Five Constraints on the Production of Culture: Law, Technology, Market, Organizational Structure and Occupational Careers." *Journal of Popular Culture* 16, no. 2 (1982): 143-153.

Pike, Dave and Tim Brown. "Till the Mummers Song is Sung." *Old Friends at Christmas*. Paradise, Newfoundland: Dave Pike and Tim Brown, Cassette DPTB-196, 1996, Side B.

Pierson, Stuart. "Review of E. Annie Proulx, *The Shipping News....* (1993)." *Newfoundland Studies* 11, no. 1 (1995): 151-153.

Pocius, Gerald L. "The Mummers Song in Newfoundland: Intellectuals, Revivalists and Cultural Nativism." *Newfoundland Studies* 4, no.1 (1988): 57-85.

Preston, Michael J., M.G. Smith, and Paul Smith. "The Peace Egg Chapbook in Scotland: An Analytic Approach to the Study of Chapbooks." *The Bibliotheck* 8, no. 3 (1976): 71-90.

Preston, Michael J., M.G. Smith, and Paul Smith. *Chapbooks and Traditional Drama. Part I. Alexander and the King of Egypt.* Sheffield: Centre for English Cultural Tradition and Language, 1977.

Proulx, E. Annie. *The Shipping News*. New York: Charles Scribner's Sons, 1993.

Purity Syrup Presents "A Christmas Visit." CBC Television, December 1990a. [Advertisement].

Purity Syrup. "Stock Up Now. You Never Know Who's Going to Drop By." *The Evening Telegram*, December 10, 1990b. [Advertisement].

Quidi Vidi Brewing Company. http://www.nlbeerhistory.com/category/quidi-vidi-brewing/.

Radio Canada Nouvelles De L'Atlantique. *"Mummers in Red Brook, Newfoundland."* Broadcast January 6, 1988.

Rose, Barbara Wade. "The Rites of Winter: The Magic and Mystery of Newfoundland's Mummers." *Imperial Oil Review*, (1990): 26-30.

Russell, Kelly. "Fiddler for Hire...." *The Evening Telegram*, December 13, 1997.

St. John's Folk Arts Council. *"The Mummers Play: A workshop by Chris Brookes and Christina Smith."* The Masonic Temple, Cathedral Street, St. John's, Newfoundland, November 17, 2001. [e-mail notice: November 5, 2001].

Sandemose, Aksel. *En Sjømann går i land* Oslo: Gyldendal, 1931. [A Sailor Goes Ashore].

"shopDownhomer.com." *Downhomer* 15, no. 7 (2000): 129.

Simani. [Bud Davidge and Sim Savory]. "Any Mummers Allowed In?" 45 rpm record. 1983. Bel Air: BA 202. Side A.

Simms, Chuck. (Composed by Ron Young, musical arrangement by Roy MacCaull). "Let the Mummers In." *Chuck's Christmas Casingle*. c.1989. Brampton, Ontario: Downhome Sound DH 8901, Side A.

Smith, Paul. "Contemporary Legend on Film and Television: Some Observations." *Contemporary Legend*, ns. 2 (1999): 137-154.

Sullivan, Rose M. "Mummering at Christmas." *The Atlantic Guardian*, December 1948.

Vaughan-Jackson, Mark. "Memories of the Outport: Exhibit Captures Essence of Daily Life in Coastal Newfoundland During 1930's." *The Evening Telegram*, February 16, 1996.

Wade, James. "Christmas Mummering Tradition Focus of McClellan Exhibit." *The Sunday Telegram*, November 10, 1991.

Wareham, Ellen J. "Mummers In Brigus." *Downhomer* 11, no. 7 (1998): front cover and 2.

Watkins, Ella and Ken Watkins. "Snapshots & Stories. Mummers in June." *Downhomer* 16, no. 7 (2003): 123.

Watkins, Reg. "Mummers Party Jig." *Downhomer Presents... Newfoundland Christmas*. 1999. St. John's, Newfoundland: Avondale

Music, CD 02 50821, Track 14.

West, Eric. *Comfort and Joy: Christmas Songs of Newfoundland and Labrador*, vol. 4. Ladle Cove, Newfoundland: Vinland Music, 2002.

Widdowson, J.D.A. "Trends in the Commercialization of English Calendar Customs: A Preliminary Survey." In *Aspects of British Calendar Customs*, edited by Theresa Buckland and Juliette Wood, 23-35. Sheffield: Sheffield Academic Press for The Folklore Society, 1993.

Willis, A. Frank. "Mummer's Night in Oshawa." *Mummers Night in Oshawa: Christmas With A. Frank Willis*. Toronto: Newfoundland Records, CD NRCD-1199, 1999, Track 1.

Young, Ron. "The Newfoundland Logic Problem.... The Mummers." *Downhomer* 11, no. 7 (1998): 47.

—. "The Newfoundland Logic Problem.... Five Mummers." *Downhomer* 16, no. 7 (2003): 141.

CHAPTER SIX

EMBODIED AND DIRECT EXPERIENCE IN PERFORMANCE STUDIES

JANE BACON

I do not know where I will begin. I only know that I am not drawn to tell the story, that I am not interested in linear evolution, that in this field there are others and no others. I allow myself to settle and be drawn into experience. Stand still and re-member. Tricky, vague territory…from, in, beyond…. a field where the primacy of rational thinking processes press the body into the shadows. How can I speak? How can I write? "To write performance," as Della Pollock says, "is not in and of itself to betray it" the betrayal "consists in not writing."[1] She goes on to explore how we might write more and to allow our textuality/writing to perform:

> to write in excess of norms of scholarly representation, to write beyond textuality into what might be called social mortalities, to make writing/textuality speak to, of, and through pleasure, possibility, disappearance, and even pain. In other words, to make writing perform.[2]

But what if, writing performance, writing the dancing body, writing performing is also an act of representation that requires a story to be told and the story of the body performing/writing is yet to be known?

> "It's difficult to get our minds round the notion of body's knowing."
> "Bodies both know and don't know."
> "Yes, both at same time."

In this article I will outline and contemplate aspects of my performance practice in an attempt to consider the invitation offered by the editors of

---

[1] Della Pollock, "Performing Writing," in The Ends of Performance, ed. Jill Lane and Peggy Phelan (New York: New York University Press, 1998), 79.
[2] Ibid.

this collection: Where has 30 years of (broad spectrum) performance studies got us in looking at the amateur, traditional, popular, particular, local, folkloric, fakeloric, competitive, unfashionable and nearly forgotten to scholarship? Along the way I hope to refocus issues of representation and performativity toward experience and embodiment.

My premise is simple: by speaking and writing the doing I may be writing performance but, more importantly, I am giving primacy to the experience and, by default, to things of and from the (my) body.[3] But potentially, unless we are conscious of it, we may be simply falling foul of a Cartesian split that has haunted western philosophy and other discourses since the Enlightenment. I would say that to put movement, action, sensation or experience into words is much more than writing performance[4] or performing writing.[5] It invites us into the world of the sensuous, sentient being-ness of our animistic ground and from here we find a heightened attentiveness and particularised expression in/of the (my) body, the (my) self, as the (my) locus of thought and action. And that takes effort; effort to note and listen to the habits, sensations and articulations of the (my) body; effort for the (my) words that might arise from such embodied attentiveness to come to the fore. Yes, effort, and practice, and time (for both writer and reader). And even then language and experience, whilst connected, are not the same.

In a 2010 article for *Gender Forum Online* I tried to articulate something of my experience of making my most recent installation "Sitting Practice"[6] which was a video and text based piece. This wasn't an attempt to write *about,* or to write performance or for the performing to write itself. I wanted to explore writing *from.* In other words my interest was to create a subjective, experiential, or phenomenological account of the creative process. I wanted to write *from* the lived and direct experience of the creative research process. It is as if I crouch down low on my haunches where I feel the gravity of the earth, know my relationship to the

---

[3] I am aware of the phenomenological implications of this particularly in the work of Husserl and Merleau-Ponty but that is not the primary focus of this article.
[4] Ronald J. Pelias, Writing Performance: Poeticizing the Researcher's Body (Carbondale, Ill: Southern Illinois University Press, 1999).
[5] Pollock, "Performing Writing."
[6] Jane Bacon, "Sitting Practice: Reflections on a Woman's Creative Process," Gender Forum, Women and Performance, issue 31 (2010): 1-5, edited by Anna Furse. http://www.genderforum.org/issues/gender-and-performance/sitting-walking-practice, 2013.

world through my experiential being and from here allow language to emerge. Perhaps I imagine in myself a two million year old self who is a microcosm of the evolution of language.[7] In one moment of writing I find myself longing to utter, struggling for sound or image, and finally words emerge. They tumble onto the page in the twenty first century as an attempt to communicate what is deeply felt from this place of habitation. This approach has developed over the past fifteen years as a methodological approach to contemporary performance making and, in particular, to practice-led research in performance. Here is an extract from that article:

> Here is a space and place where I can be present with the ebbs and flows, with the processes of my creative spirit, to a giving over to my embodied felt and imaged experience. *Stop again...*
>
> *Another beginning...*Eventually I am running toward the sea, the sky opens out into the sea and my vision expands with each pace. Time, I hear ego saying, there isn't enough of it...then something more arrives and the "problem" of my life is expanded and scattered about the landscape as imagination takes hold...who is here?
> Seeing who is here is sometimes a more difficult thing to do than could possibly be imagined...
> So what am I doing on this contemplative walk, in this sitting practice, in these poetics and images? Perhaps a word I am searching for is *process,* an artistic process imaged in both inner and outer realities. It is not the product created but the process of creation that enlivens.[8]

In my own research journey I have moved from dancer to ethnographer and on to performance maker/writer. Kirsten Hastrup, whose comments are based on her experience of working with Odin Teatret, says "[t]o represent the body as the locus of action, we must first realise that the art of performing, dramatically or culturally, cannot be studied independently of the performing body. One does not have a body, one is a body."[9] I am my body, my body is me. I may write about my body but that is not to write about me. I can write from my body and that is both to write from me and what I perceive to be not me. To move from a body-centred notion of practice we need an agent, we need to acknowledge the ghost in the

---

[7] Anthony Stevens, Two Million Year Old Self (Texas: Texas A&M Press, 1993).
[8] Bacon, "Sitting Practice."
[9] Kirsten Hastrup, A Passage to Anthropology: Between Experience and Theory (London: Routledge, 1995), 90.

machine, stop talking about "the" body and embrace "my" body. We need to breathe life into her, she is a living body, a person. And she experiences the world of "not me" through and in relation to the world at large. And this means that we embrace both subjective and objective positions of self and other.

And this is the problem of a writing or performing practice that is dis-embodied then followed by an over bodification, which is not just present in the writing of performance but in performance research itself. This is and always will be a dialectical relationship between self and other, subject and object which Performance Studies struggles to hold. Built on the deconstruction of textualism, Performance Studies is still a writerly enterprise that produces texts "grounded in the distinctive styles, rhythms, idioms, and personal identities of local folk and vernacular culture."[10] In its textual troubling is another hegemonic sleight-of-hand. The body has become our text. Performance Studies scholar Diana Taylor, suggests that Performance Studies is unique not because of what it *is* but because of "what it allows us to *do*." But her "doing" refers to a "theoretical lens for a sustained historical analysis of performance practices."[11] Once again the textual analysis takes the foreground and the doing falls into the shadows of an object of study. But if we follow Conquergood's question, "What kinds of knowledge are privileged or displaced when performed experience becomes a way of knowing, a method of critical enquiry, a mode of understanding?"[12] then we begin to open up new territories of experience. In this landscape it becomes possible to enquire as to the whereabouts of the one who writes when the writing is all about the style or constructed identity? I continue to be the one who crouches low to the ground feeling the power of the world as well as being the (my) body that feels the gravity as it pulls and holds me firm in the grip of its power. I struggle on and work to hold the tension of subjective and objective positions.

---

[10] Norman K. Denzin, *Performance Ethnography: Critical Pedagogy and the Politics of Culture* (Thousand Oaks; London; New Delhi: Sage Publications, 2003), 123, quoted in Brian Rusted, "Introduction: From Ethnography of Performance to Performance Ethnography," Canadian Theatre Review 151, (2012): 5.

[11] Diana Taylor, "Performance Studies and Hemispheric Focus," in Performance Studies: An Introduction, by Richard Schechner (New York: Routledge, 2002), 7.

[12] Dwight Conquergood, "Rethinking Ethnography: Towards a Critical Cultural Politics," Communication Monographs 58, (1991): 190.

I wonder if these perspectives are not all interconnected and interrelated in their emergence from the ephemeral nature of performance, the intuitive creative process and the difficulty of finding suitable means to articulate "doing." Research that works from and with the bodymind environment[13] in embodied practice-led research may just be one more of those interconnections. Discussion and debate about practice-led research has been around for many years and the discipline of performance studies has gone some way to inscribing action and doing with a value in the academy that it previously may not have had. But it seems to me that young researchers still have the same questions and concerns. In some respects, I tell them, it is so much easier to write about the other. When the subject of study is one and the same as the one conducting the research then we become blind whilst at the same time thinking we can see more clearly than anyone else. And there is a danger that our sense of inner knowing might be mistaken for insight or new knowledge that develops our discipline.

So let me get to my point—self and other as creative source. Fundamental to this is the role of lived and direct experience. We are sentient beings and our way of being in the world is guided by our body, our libidinal energy. And this is complex territory. Of course, in academia, the body has not had a place of primacy until recently. The body has been despised, mistrusted, and rejected as the source of our solipsism, narcissism, carnality and more. But research in dance and performance practice involves (my) body and (my) body moving must be articulate in a way that illuminates the creative process and product as well as furthering the discipline we call dance and performance studies. If I allow myself to fall foul of the projection of the body as object then I lose an opportunity to explore what (my) body knows and how that knowledge can be brought into the realm of language. I am not one of those practitioner academics who believes that the dance can stand alone and offer its own meaning without recourse to language. It may be that bringing an experience into the realm of language, into words, in and of itself, according to Cognitive Scientist Schooler, introduces a disruption into experience that fundamentally alters that experience.[14] So language is our problem and our imperative but only so far as we think of human language as something unique. As Abram so evocatively writes of language, "we share it...with

---

[13] Antonio Damasio, Descartes' error: Emotion, Reason and the Human Brain (New York: Harper Collins, 1994).
[14] Jonathan W. Schooler, "Verbalization produces a transfer inappropriate processing shift," Journal of Applied Cognitive Psychology 16, no. 8 (2002): 989-997.

the mutter and moan of the wind."[15] Language is all around us and our capacity to write our experiences is an opportunity to remember how we came to language and our need to communicate with and in relationship to the world.

We in the world of dance and performance studies like to declaim the wonders of knowledge that comes from the body and this means finding language that speaks of and from the body. This is a wonderful turn in the academy although I also wonder at our need to place our bodies in a place of such importance. But still it is refreshing to see somatics and the body being embraced in all manner of discourses from philosophy to cognitive science, anthropology, sociology and psychology. But I am also aware of the danger and the deep unconscious of the body and am not suggesting that the body per se holds a magic key. Mine is not a body-centric but a bodymind treatise. Recent research in neuroscience is beginning to support this approach. McGilchrist[16] suggests that the right hemisphere of our brains offers a poetic, imaginative, associative, emotional type of thinking. This, interestingly enough, can be linked to the work of the depth psychologist C. G. Jung who,

> without knowing it […] advocated a therapeutic approach which was predominantly right hemispheric—it had to be in order to counter the left hemispheric biases of Western society…wholeness entailed the "union of opposites"…it was all a question of balance.[17]

McGilchrist also says that Enlightenment thinking has encouraged the dominance of left brain activity but that this cultural emphasis is creating a paucity of experience as creativity and intuition are not encouraged. The left brain offers logic and reasoning. But the brain operates as a complex organism even though McGilchrist suggests that we are becoming more and more left-brain dominant. The left hemisphere most typically processes narrow focused information, to do with our needs, and is adept at verbal reasoning. The right hemisphere processes information of a broad open nature directed toward what is going on in the world beyond

---

[15] David Abram, Becoming Animal: An Earthy Cosmology (New York: Vintage, 2010), 12.
[16] Iain McGilchrist, The Master and his Emissary: The Divided Brain and the Making of the Western World (New Haven, CN: Yale University Press, 2009).
[17]Anthony Stevens, Archetype: A Natural History of the Self (London: Routledge and Kegan Paul, 1982), 275.

ourselves. And other research supports this. Daniel Kahneman,[18] for example, in his *Thinking, Fast and Slow*, suggests the "experiencing self" and the "remembering self" are systems of thinking that might be associated with a "fast" and "slow" thinking. The "fast" could be said to be similar to Jung's definition of "intuition"[19] but also to a bodily sense of knowing that comes quickly and without reason or careful logic. The "slow" is similar to Jung's "directed thinking"[20] and appears to link to McGilchrist's understanding of the role and function of "left" brain activity. But where is our feeling function in this research and where is our body?

A rational, objective intellect, I would argue, is not sufficient to conduct creative performance research but requires feeling along with the poetic, imaginative and associative and, a body aware process. Hillman warns us that in this age of feeling where all therapists say "how do you feel about that," there is a massive difference between having feelings and using feelings. "Feelings are not only personal; they reflect historical and universal phenomena."[21] So I am suggesting that body and feeling in our research offers us a way to understand how our consciousness uses feelings and how feelings are operating in our unconscious. I may feel as if my body *has* feelings but it is *me* who has these feelings. Part of a conscious research process may often include learning how to *use* these feelings.

Damasio[22] explores the role of feeling (as distinguished from emotions) on brain functioning and says that thinking is not simply located in the head, regardless of the type of thinking, but also in the many neural pathways throughout the body which are activated in processes of

---

[18] Daniel Kahneman, Thinking, Fast and Slow (New York: Farrar, Straus and Giroux, 2011).

[19] Carl G. Jung, "Four Psychological Types," in Collected Works vol. 6., by Carl G. Jung, 2nd ed. (Princeton NJ: Princeton University Press, 1971 [1921]).

[20] Carl G. Jung, "Two kinds of thinking," in Symbols of Transformation: Collected Works vol. 5., by Carl G. Jung, 2nd ed. (Princeton NJ: Princeton University Press, 1967), 7-33.

[21] James Hillman, "The Feeling Function," in Lectures on Jung's Typology, ed. Marie-Louise von Franz and James Hillman (Woodstock, CN: Spring Publications, 1998), 99.

[22] Damasio, *Descartes' error.*, see also Antonio Damasio, The Feeling of What Happens: Body, Emotion and the Making of Consciousness (London: Vintage, 2000); Antonio Damasio, Self Comes to Mind: Constructing the Conscious Brain (New York: Vintage: 2012).

perception and cognition. He suggests that these "somatic markers" give us vital information that aid our decision making processes. This is similar to the "felt sense" as defined by psychologist Eugene Gendlin.[23] The felt-sense, according to Gendlin, is always present and available to us. If we allow ourselves time to dwell in "felt-sense" —prior to moving to interpretation or meaning—it may offer new ways of thinking. If we place Damasio, Gendlin and McGilchrist together we find that all kinds of thinking must and do, either consciously or unconsciously, involve body and mind or as Damasio[24] calls it a "bodymind environment." Our different modes of apprehending the world may often seem incompatible but left and right brain, and body-brain, do not function independently but as a whole. Our thinking mind also has a feeling mind which incorporates our sensorial experience. Our instinctual body is also a thinking body. The human organism is a complexity of inter-connected systems and functions.

These scientific findings are concurrent with Jung's view that no psychological change could happen unless the individual felt it in their body, or had an emotional response to the experience.

> When the great swing has taken an individual into the world of symbolic mysteries, nothing comes of it, nothing can come of it, unless it has been associated with the earth, unless it has happened when that individual was in the body...And so individuation can only take place if you first return to the body, to your earth, only then does it become true.[25]

Jung was deeply committed to exploring the inter-relationship between body, mind and spirit and this sometimes took him into wild and esoteric researches. In his lifelong research into alchemy he discovered the alchemist's idea that man was "a microcosm, representing in all his parts the earth or the universe, is a remnant of an original psychic identity which reflected a twilight state of consciousness."[26] It was, according to Jung, an image of how earlier humans thought about the role of the individual in relation to the Almighty, but it also attests to the Oneness of man and spirit.

---

[23] Eugene T. Gendlin, Focusing (London: Bentam Press, 1978).

[24] Damasio, The Feeling of.

[25] Carl G. Jung, The visions seminars vol. 2. (New York: Spring Publications, 1976 [1934]), 473.

[26] Carl G. Jung, Commentary on the "Secret of the Golden Flower," in Collected Works vol. 13., by Carl G. Jung (Princeton NJ: Princeton University Press, 1967 [1929]), par. 122.

Man is to be esteemed a little world, and in all respects he is to be compared to a world. The bones under his skin are likened to mountains, for by them is the body strengthened, even as the earth is by rocks, and the flesh is taken for earth, and the great blood vessels for great rivers, and the little ones for small streams that pour into the great rivers. The bladder is the sea, wherein the great as well as the small streams congregate. The hair is compared to sprouting herbs, the nails on the hands and feet, and whatever else may be discovered inside and outside a man, all according to its kind is compared to the world.[27]

Jung knew through his research into alchemy, eastern philosophies and other aspects of human endeavour of an earthly intelligence and of the fragility of our current assumption that we are in control of our lives and our world. But the alchemists also believed that the mark of a spiritual man was his self-knowledge and knowledge of God and to know God one must work to differentiate between the earth-bound, fleshly man (Thoth) who contained within him the spiritual man, whose name is light.[28] It was the inner, spiritual man, the alchemists sought to set free. So, how to "set free" the spirit of our research without losing our "matter"? How to be of the earth and from the earth and find our spirit there rather than falling for the legacy of Christianity that leaves us with in an assumption upwards and away from the body? Jung tells us that when the mystics "descend into the depths of their own being they find 'in their heart' the image of the sun, they find their own life-force which they call the 'sun' for a legitimate, and I would say, a *physical* reason, because our source of energy and life actually *is* the sun."[29] When we work from the premise that we find our own gods and goddesses in our body and mind, both conscious and unconscious, then we have access to our life force. Perhaps I imagine this life force to be a part of our mode of apprehending the world. Our sensate awareness of phenomenal experience becomes a space of creativity and imagination. Could it be that our internal world becomes our creative research and our mode of apprehending the world becomes our methodology?

According to Avens, the history of philosophy and science in the west since Kant is an attempt to "convert all things...into controllable objects

---

[27] Ibid.

[28] Ibid., par.125-6.

[29] Carl G. Jung, "The Tavistock lectures: on the theory and practice of analytical psychology: Lecture 1," in Collected Works vol. 18. by Carl G. Jung (Princeton NJ: Princeton University Press, 1976), par.176. Emphasis original.

for a subject"[30] —including the human soul. Here is the attempt to name and label all things including bodily experience. Here, the Cartesian shift to mind from psyche is apparent, the body becomes the tool for the all-powerful mind; the soul, previously embraced by the term psyche is no longer part of the physician's concern. From our western, enlightenment tradition, it is our minds, our ego position that has a forward impulse, but so too does the instinct; our libidinal energy is a life force that is life itself but perhaps we too often confuse and conflate our need for progress and "to know" as researchers? These are struggles with that which we cannot or do not "know" or that which we cannot explain, label or pathologise. We are often longing for something but the labelling is a reifying, a fixing of meaning that often floats free of the body.

Perhaps this new way of working with the (my) body as creative source for our research processes is revealing a deeper concern. Is it that more and more young researchers are longing to explicate something that feels inexplicable? They often seem to be searching for something they do not yet know, searching for the unknown. In my experience, they do not usually attach themselves to any organised religion or preconceived myth, or even to a singular philosophical or ideological stance.[31] So, what happens if we look into the azure blue of their longing? James Hillman[32] tells us that the colour blue in dreams and experience, the azure blue, is a longing but we mistake this as a longing *for* something. If we can simply hold our longing in our bodies long enough we begin to allow it the space and time needed for its growth and development. It is not the longing *for*...but the *longing* itself. It is not the arrival but the journey that must concern us.

My methodological approach to practice-led research is processual in that my attention always drifts to the processes of engagement, of lived experience or direct experience rather than to the objects, products or material of any given situation. It began with ethnography and a desire to know more about the other. I wanted to know what role dancing was playing in the meaning making of people's lives. On a long journey to discover the answer to this question the tables were soon turned and the

---

[30] Roberts Avens, Imagination is Reality: Western Nirvana in Jung, Hillman, Barfield and Cassirer (Dallas TX: Spring Publications, 1980), 15.
[31] Jane Bacon, "The voice of her body: somatic practices as a basis for creative research methodology," Dance and Somatics Journal 2, no. 1 (2010): 63-74.
[32] James Hillman, Alchemical Psychology (Putnam Conn.: Springs Publications, 2010).

very people I was asking the questions began to ask me the same questions. "What do you want from us? You came into our world and we opened our hearts to you. You are implicated in this research now too whether you like it or not. Why do you come to our dance class? What is it we have that you so need? This is important to you too, but how?" I was shocked. Stunned. These English Arabic dancers seemed "other" to me. They were involved in neo-paganism, worshipped the Earth Goddess Isis and believed that Arabic dancing was a vehicle for expression of their essential femininity. My radical feminist self could see nothing of me in that. Yet, they thought they could see something in me that I could not see myself. Even if I was dubious, I was being asked to look inward, to reconsider their "otherness" by looking to my inner self. So, after a lot of shock and confusion, I decided I would begin to ask the same questions of myself.[33] I undertook a self-ethnography that turned into a ten year process and took me on a journey which at first seemed to be away from my beginnings as an ethnographer and performer but eventually brought me full circle—not to ethnography or performance per se but to the subject of spirituality and femininity (but that is another story).

The result was that I was soon labelled as a maker of autobiographical performance. In 2005, Dorothy Max Prior, in *Total Theatre Magazine*, coined the phrase "self as source" as an attempt to define what she had broadly called autobiographical performance.[34] But I wasn't interested to tell the story of my life. I was interested in what I did not yet know, in stories I did not have access to. I wanted to explore how to articulate what the (my) body knows. In some ways this was a search for new meaning but also to escape from meaning and representation. No chance. The search for meaning occurs in the bodymind environment[35] and goes beyond discourse and narrative, although it is an inescapable fact that the body aids our meaning making through its fleshy presence and gesture, in liminal spaces where meanings are more closely conceived as belief systems. These deeply held and embodied systems course through my veins giving meaning and hope to each day that I visit the studio or take up my position at the computer. Through my lived experience of "who I am" I am able to delve into what I know to be "dance and performance studies research."

---

[33] Joann Kealiinohomoku, Theory and Methods for an Anthropological Study of Dance (Flagstaff, Arizona: Cross-Cultural Dance Resources, 2008).
[34] Dorothy Max Prior, "I am I, The Self as the Source: Dorothy Max Prior looks at Autobiography," Total Theatre Magazine 17, Issue 2 (2005): no page.
[35] Damasio, *Descartes' error*.

This theoretical and practical interest leads me to explore the ways in which the dancing body I have is also the person I am. I imagine this processual approach to be like Donald Winnicott's "indwelling" of the psyche in the soma. It is an invitation to participate in a twenty-first century, postmodern take on a psycho-somatic experience of *unity*. For Winnicott this is a process by which the infant becomes a person in a body, an individual in her own right, albeit unconsciously. The psyche "indwells" within the soma, linking motor, sensory, and functional experience with the infant's new state of being a person.[36] Further, there comes into existence what might be called a "membrane," which we can equate with the surface of the skin and this makes a position between the infant's "me" and "not me." So the infant comes to have an inside, and outside, and a body scheme.[37] What follows is the baby's potential to have an internal world of its own, or it moves from a phase of holding to being in relationship with-Self and other. In Winnicott's terms the child begins to play and discover that I AM because, mother/father/carer is Not me. Could this also be the case in our research? When I begin to understand my research as Not me it is also the moment when I begin to know that I AM. Or have I just unraveled my argument? No matter, I like this. It brings me back to self and other. This likens the research process to a child's development where the parent researcher allows the child research to become without imposition.

To research without imposition asks us to "notice"[38] the "vague"[39] or to believe that Damasio is right and that our bodymind environment has more to offer than the thinking mind can allow. In all of this there is a both/and, a place where moving becomes witnessing, performer becomes audience, self becomes other and so on. The integral creativity that emerges without imposition can be attended to, cared for and cultivated. It is akin to watching the sun rise, a flower bloom or the wings of a bird hover on the air. It often emerges in a tenuous space between conscious and unconscious aspects of Self, between Self and Other (inter-subjectivity). In each of these dyadic exchanges I attempt to allow for an expansion of knowledge, a creativity, that might emerge out of dimly perceived relations and objects in a place where mind and body are more

---

[36] Donald W. Winnicott, "The theory of the parent-child relationship," International Journal of Psychoanalysis 41, (1960): 585-595.
[37] Ibid.
[38] Gendlin, *Focusing*.
[39] William James, The Principles of Psychology, 2 vols (London: Dover, 1950 [1890]).

in tune with our animal selves[40] but in a physical and experiential rather than conceptual way.

But what if we are all elsewhere, present in the past, and lost in the present. Economist Donald Kahneman says we are always prey to our remembering selves. Even in this moment, here and now, we are both engaging with this experience—you reading, me writing—in order to remember. We are both present and yet as I sit and write you are future and as you read I am past. In this moment we both transcend time. If I work to allow my experiencing self more resonance in my present moment then perhaps my remembering self will allow an expansion of what is known to me. Perhaps I will begin to dream into your present? Might this require a slowing down, a stillness and silence that invites us inward and outward, to notice our essential being and becoming-ness in a world of wonder, awe and the "shudder" of the numinous?

I embrace self and other, I embrace becoming, I long for the possibility and potential of the "shudder" as constructs of an external and internal reality and also want to allow for space *between* where all binaries and dialectics dissolve. In between the opposites, Jung suggests, might emerge a "third thing" from the transcendent function.[41] This is something that was not known before and may be experienced as more than the original "this" or "that." It is also similar to what Otto[42] calls the "shudder" of the numinous or what Kant, Schopenhauer and Hegel refer to as the awe of the sublime. This is a creative process and it is a deeply rooted bodily experience of (my) Other. As Buddhist and photographer, John Daido Loori says "the creative process, like a spiritual journey, is intuitive, non-linear, and experiential. It points us toward our essential nature, which is a reflection of the boundless creativity of the universe."[43]

Maybe this is what author Sara Maitland was writing about in *A Book of Silence* (2009). In documenting her journey to discover silence Maitland suggests there are two kinds of searching for silence, one which shores up

---

[40] Gilles Deleuze and Félix Guattari, Kafka Towards a Minor Literature. Trans. Dana Polan (Minneapolis and London: University of Minnesota Press, 1975).
[41] Carl G. Jung, The transcendent function. Trans. Alexander R. Pope (Zürich: Student Association, C.G. Jung Institute, 1957).
[42] Rudolf Otto, The Idea of the Holy (London: Oxford University, 1958 [1923]).
[43] John D. Loori, The Zen of Creativity: Cultivating Your Artistic Life (New York: Ballantine Books, 2005), 1.

the ego boundaries and one which is a non-boundaried encounter that invites the Other. She continues

> I have come…to use the terms "permeable" and "boundaried" selves, or identities, to sum up the two positions […] In the West, we tend to see "normal," healthy people as firmly, though not excessively, boundaried. Permeable selves…tend to be less rationalist and less atomised…a modern narrative will say that anyone who lets the (divine or delusional) Other too far in, who weakens their own boundaries, or has them weakened, is "mad"…[w]hile in a religious or spiritual narrative will tend to sense that those who will not consent to be used by the forces of the Other are the mad ones.[44]

Perhaps the search for silence, as described by Maitland, articulates the human desire for experiences beyond our ego selves. In a space where expanded consciousness, the vague and the felt are encouraged and embraced, mover and witness or performer and audience or subject and object are called into an engagement with one another in a manner that is more akin to entering the dream world. This is a space where looking becomes seeing, where our felt experiences might help us to stay with the image and "let it give us what it bears."[45] But we can only do this if we maintain a distinction between "inherent significance" and "interpretive meaning," what Hillman would call the distinction between "insighting an image" and hermeneutics. I gently, silently work with the distinctive matter of the (my) bodily and in the territory of the "bodymind" in order to be able to "feel" my way in the dark allowing *something* to emerge. The search for silence and this research process speaks to a search for realignment to something not yet known and yet I am unconcerned by the notion, in and of itself, of "new knowledge." I am interested in a creative and artistic research imperative that exists in many and drives some of us. This is a *not yet known-ness* which we encounter when searching for our research aims or questions. Each moment of practice as research is a moment of self-creation. As research our dancing and performing is another developmental stage in life, it is a performed process, and my interest is to stop long enough to notice the fullness of each moment.

So my job is not a programme of work with the internal images where ego trawls for meaning: it is more an attitude of giving over to the images

---

[44] Sara Maitland, A Book of Silence: A Journey in Search of the Pleasures and Power of Silence (London: Granta, 2009), 252-253.

[45] James Hillman, The Essential James Hillman: A Blue Fire (London: Routledge, 1990), 60.

and cultivating them for their own sake, like Gendlin's "noticing"[46] that can give rise to something that we previously had no language to articulate. And so I guess I am trying to explore what happens when I bring this perspective into the world and try to "allow" from the noticing and cultivate what I call research for its own sake. For me this is a process of therapeutic, artistic and spiritual significance. Here is a space and place where I can be present with the ebbs and flows, with the processes of my creative spirit, to a giving over to my embodied felt and imaged experience.

In all these processes described there is, for me, a sense that the grasping of and attending to direct and lived experience might allow me, and others, to speak as both subject and object of my research. I hope this might be a move beyond this duality whilst embracing its linguistic inescapability. I suggest to those I work with that to become the subject of your research means you know and work consciously with your practice as both self and other. You are both "dancer/ maker/ researcher" of this specific project *and* the project itself.

With my embodied self I have the power and potential access to a "being" or a mindful "noticing" of felt experience[47] and there we have the powerful beginnings of a methodology for practice as research in dance and performance and for the contemporary performance ethnographer. This is not a suggestion that a focus on "embodied self" will provide a unitary self, a knowing self, an undividedness—no, it will provide a frame through which agency and alterity can be embraced, where process is understood as developmental as well as performative, where writing performing is also performing writing, where we *are* and can work *with* both self and other—all present and available to an observing/witnessing self/other we call "researcher."

And finally, I believe that it is our responsibility, as holders of positions in academia, to develop and further our discipline and make it as fully available to future generations as possible. But I also suggest we often continue to struggle against struggle itself and we might do well (or maybe this is just for me) to let go of striving toward a goal, toward the clear intention to create "performance." My attempts at creating movement, image, poetics are failures. My attempt to impose my perspective into the

---

[46] Gendlin, *Focusing*.
[47] Ibid.

discipline of performance studies is a failure. But I continue to long for an expansion of "knowledge" that might emerge from this particular kind of attention. I pay attention to the "vague," the "felt," in the hope that it does not slip away, I attempt to hold the tension of the opposites. But of course, it always and forever slips, slides, disappears, reappears and transforms. Such is the beauty of the process. I seek illumination to creatively articulate experience. I sit and I wait.

> In my dreaming of the Other
> I find my Self
> In a space
> Between
> A deep longing
> Takes shape
> It's quality—breathtaking—
> I long for you
> My Other
> Self

Works Cited

Abram, David. *Becoming Animal: An Earthly Cosmology*. New York: Vintage, 2010.

Avens, Roberts. *Imagination is Reality: Western Nirvana in Jung, Hillman, Barfield and Cassirer*. Dallas, TX: Spring Publications, 2003.

Bacon, Jane. "Sitting Practice: Reflections on a Woman's Creative Process." *Gender Forum, Women and Performance* 31, (2010a): 1-5. edited by Anna Furse. http://www.genderforum.org/issues/gender-and-performance/sitting-walking-practice, 2013

—. "The voice of her body: somatic practices as a basis for creative research methodology." *Dance and Somatics Journal* 2, no. 1 (2010b): 63-74.

Conquergood, Dwight. "Rethinking Ethnography: Towards a Critical Cultural Politics." *Communications Monographs* 58, (1991): 179-94.

Damasio, Antonio *Descartes' error: Emotion, Reason, and the Human Brain*. New York: Harper Collins, 1994.

—. *The Feeling of What Happens: Body, Emotion and the Making of Consciousness*. London: Vintage, 2000.

—. *Self Comes to Mind: Constructing the Conscious Brain*. New York: Vintage, 2012.

Deleuze, Gilles, and Félix Guattari. *Kafka: Towards a Minor Literature.* Trans. Dana Polan. Minneapolis and London: University of Minnesota, 1975.

—. *A Thousand Plateaus.* Trans. Brian Massumi. London: Continuum, 2004. [1980.]

Denzin, Norman K. *Performance Ethnography: Critical Pedagogy and the Politics of Culture*, 123. Thousand Oaks; London; New Delhi: Sage Publications, 2003. Quoted in Brian Rusted, "Introduction: From Ethnography of Performance to Performance Ethnography." Canadian Theatre Review 151, (2012): 5.

Gendlin, Eugene T. *Focusing.* London: Bantam Press, 1978.

Hastrup, Kirsten. *A Passage to Anthropology: Between Experience and Theory.* London: Routledge, 1999.

Hillman, James. "The Feeling Function." in *Lectures on Jung's Typology*, edited by Marie-Louise von Franz and James Hillman. Woodstock, CN: Spring Publications, 1986.

—. *The Essential James Hillman: A Blue Fire.* London: Routledge, 1990.

—. *Alchemical Psychology.* Putnam, Conn: Spring Publications, 2010.

James, William. *The Principles of Psychology* 2 vols. London: Dover, 1950. [1890.]

Jung, Carl G. "The Tavistock lectures: on the theory and practice of analytical psychology. Lecture 1." In *Collected Works* vol. 18., by Carl G. Jung, 5-35. Princeton NJ: Princeton University Press, 1976.

—. "Two kinds of thinking." In *Symbols of Transformation: Collected Works* vol. 5., by Carl G. Jung, 2nd ed., 7-33. Princeton NJ: Princeton University Press, 1967.

—. "The Structure and Dynamics of the Psyche." In *Collected Works* vol. 8. Trans. R.F. Hull. edited by Sir Herbert Read, Michael Fordham and Gerhard Adler. London: Routledge, 1960.

—. *The transcendent function.* Trans. Alexander R. Pope. Zürich: Student association, C.G. Jung Institute, 1957.

—. *The Visions Seminars* vol. 2. New York: Spring Publications, 1976. [1934.]

—. "Commentary on 'The Secret of the golden flower.'" *Collected Works* vol. 13., by Carl G. Jung, 1-56. Princeton NJ: Princeton University Press, 1967. [1929.]

—. "Four Psychological Types." *Collected Works* vol. 6, by Carl G. Jung, 2nd ed. Princeton NJ: Princeton University Press, 1971. [1929.]

Kahneman, Daniel. *Thinking, Fast and Slow.* New York: Farrar, Straus and Giroux, 2011.

Kealiinohomoku, Joann. *Theory and Methods for an Anthropological Study of Dance*. Flagstaff, Arizona: Cross-Cultural Dance Resources, 2008.

Loori, John D. *The Zen of Creativity: Cultivating your Artistic Life*. New York: Ballantine Books, 2005.

Maitland, Sara. *A Book of Silence: A Journey in Search of the Pleasures and Power of Silence*. London: Granta, 2009.

McGilchrist, Iain. *The Master and his Emissary: The Divided Brain and the Making of the Western World*. New Haven, CN: Yale University Press, 2009.

Otto, Rudolf. *The Idea of the Holy*. London: Oxford University, 1958. [1923.]

Pelias, Ronald J. *Writing Performance: Poeticizing the Researcher's Body*. Carbondale, Ill: Southern Illinois University Press, 1999.

Pollock, Della. "Performing Writing." In *The Ends of Performance*, edited by Jill Lane and Peggy Phelan, 73-103. New York: New York University, 1988.

Prior, Dorothy Max. "I am I, The Self as the Source: Dorothy Max Prior looks at Autobiography in Performance." *Total Theatre Magazine* 17, Issue 2 (2005): no page.

Schooler, Jonathan W. "Verbalization produces a transfer inappropriate processing shift." *Journal of Applied Cognitive Psychology* 16, no. 8 (2002): 989-997.

Stevens, Anthony. *Archetype: A Natural History of the Self*. London: Routledge and Keegan Paul, 1982.

—. *Two Million Year Old Self*. Texas: Texas A&M Press, 1993.

Taylor, Diana. "Performance Studies, A Hemispheric Focus." In *Performance Studies: An Introduction*, by Richard Schechner, 7-8. New York: Routledge, 2002.

Winnicott, Donald W. "The theory of the parent-child relationship." *International Journal of Psychoanalysis* 41, (1960): 585-595.

CHAPTER SEVEN

AUTO-ETHNOGRAPHY
AND DISSOLVING DICHOTOMIES:
SOME NOTES ON THE 'SHIFT' FORMAT
AT PERFORMANCE STUDIES INTERNATIONAL

KAREN QUIGLEY

I am attending Performance Studies international's 18th conference, at the University of Leeds in June 2012. The title of this conference is "performance—culture—industry," and it's a Saturday afternoon, the fourth day of five. I am sitting in an afternoon panel in a studio, a sort of black box performance space with windows along one wall, out of which we can see both the uncharacteristically bright sun, and the inappropriately dressed teenagers hanging around outside the student union building. Inappropriately-dressed for the weather, that is. It's warm and muggy both outside and in, but the devotees of Ghostfest, a metal and hardcore music festival taking place at the University of Leeds alongside (though unrelated to) Performance Studies international's (PSi) annual conference, are clad in black, leather, and heavy boots. Waiting for the panel to start, I absent-mindedly wonder what might happen if the events were more inter-related, if there could be some sort of package deal whereby the Ghostfest festival pass also entitles the bearer to enter the conference spaces, and vice versa. For example, I've just come to this panel from the Unnamed Room in the Baines Wing of the University, where Alan Read from King's College London has been sitting since early morning, reading aloud in half-hour increments from the novel he has been writing in recent years. *The White Estuary*, Read's programme note informs us, "is a novel that grew out of a footnote," an autobiographical wondering about lateness and the posthumous, "an unreliable memoir."[1] In a dimly lit room we join him

---

[1] Alan Read, "Programme note for *The White Estuary*" (Handout distributed by the author, Performance Studies international, Leeds, UK, June, 2012).

in tracing this "landscape of [his] experience," curtains drawn, the
audience in comfortable chairs, listening to Read's voice alongside the
instrumental music of Bert Kaempfert.[2] Perhaps, for the delegates of
Ghostfest, some time in the Unnamed Room would be a welcome contrast
to bands such as "Bleed From Within" and "Breaking Point," the
aggressive names chiming in an unconsciously interesting way with
questions being raised at this year's PSi conference around the idea of our
work as performance practitioners, scholars, and teachers; what we say
when someone asks "What do you do?"; when "work" stops; how many
hours a week we "work" and so on.[3] In an exchange, it might be
interesting for Read and others to join the throngs at the performance of
one of Saturday's headline acts at Ghostfest, "Brutality Will Prevail"
perhaps with the 2014 Research Excellence Framework in mind, and the
kind of "Impact" narrative that could be traced through an encounter
between senior performance studies academics and teenage metal and
hardcore fans.[4]

   However, I must leave that lightly-considered thought hanging in the
air, for two reasons. In the first place, the panel I am sitting in has started,
or rather, the "shift" I am sitting in, of which more in a moment. It's half-
past two, and Broderick Chow from Brunel University has his collaborator
Tom Wells in a wrestling-style headlock, while Louise Owen from
Birkbeck University effortlessly sings jazz tunes into a microphone, and a
metronome ticks in the background. Maybe not a typical post-lunch panel
on the penultimate day of a conference, but since 2009, this methodology
of conferencing has become an integral part of the programme at PSi.
Secondly, though I will return to other auto-ethnographical explorations of
some aspects of recent PSi conferences below, I have also been examining
these personal reflections in terms of some of the dichotomies with which
performance studies and theatre studies continue to be concerned. In this
chapter, I will trace a brief pathway through the "shift" format that has
been operating as part of the PSi annual conferences since 2009,
attempting to relate my own small spectatorial experiences of this format
to wider currents in performance studies. I have been a delegate at the
2009, 2011, and 2012 PSi conferences, and have found it interesting to
note the shift format as a welcome response to ongoing concerns about

---

[2] Ibid.
[3] EFestivals, "Ghostfest '12," EFestivals,
http://www.efestivals.co.uk/festivals/ghostfest/2012 (accessed January 31, 2013). [4]
Research Excellent Framework, http://www.ref.ac.uk/ (accessed January 31,
2013).

what the practices of performance studies might be. Drawing on Stephen Bottoms' 2003 article "The efficacy / effeminacy braid" and Peter Harrop's article "What's in a name?" from 2005, both of whom refer specifically to performance studies/theatre studies dichotomies, I want to suggest that, more recently, there has been a blurring (or perhaps re-blurring) of the line between the two fields, due in no small part to the efforts of PSi. Indeed, a possible point of reference for the beginning of this most recent (re-)blurring can be traced to the opening plenary of the 2009 conference in Zagreb, to which I will return in the conclusion to this chapter.

The place that my auto-ethnographic writing holds in this discussion is as follows. In approaching this chapter, (which grew out of a conference paper presented at the Contemporary Ethnography and Traditional Performance conference at the University of Chester in 2012), I was initially interested in the sort of personal ethnography that I could begin to map onto aspects of the changing field of performance studies over the past decade. I began my undergraduate studies in Drama and Theatre Studies in Dublin in 2003, my postgraduate studies in Text and Performance Studies in London in 2007, and in re-tracing the journey from there to here (University of Chester) and from then to now (2013), I have been wondering about the connections between my own growing awareness of key concepts in performance studies during these years, to movements in and through the discipline more generally. Of course, this trajectory stills the flux of the history of performance studies to a significant extent. For example, I do not suggest that such work continues similar examinations to those presented by either Bottoms or Harrop, though a 2003-2013 timeline certainly discusses a period of time that follows on from both. Indeed, Harrop refers to "the last ten years"[5] and Bottoms to "the last couple of decades"[6] in order to mark the history of definitions of performance studies, and the field's expansion, respectively. Rather, the project of this chapter represents a much narrower span of thinking and writing, confining its scope to a specific aspect (the shift format) of a particular event (PSi's annual conference) over the past few

---

[5] Peter Harrop, "'What's in a name?,'" Studies in Theatre and Performance 25, (2005): 193.
[6] Stephen Bottoms, "The Efficacy/Effeminacy Braid: Unpicking the Performance Studies/Theatre Studies Dichotomy," Theatre Topics 13, no. 2 (2003): 173.
[7] Jon McKenzie, Heike Roms, and C.J. W-L Wee. eds. Contesting Performance: Global Sites of Research (Basingstoke: Palgrave Macmillan, 2009), 6.

years (2009-2013) in order to consider a space where my reflective experiences can co-exist with analytical tracings of other kinds.

That said, it seems appropriate to think briefly (and broadly) through some moments in performance studies' history, in order to arrive in 2009 with a sense of what has gone before, particularly in terms of the more fluid movement between theatre studies and performance studies that has, in my opinion, been a feature of both fields over the past ten years. For example, Jon McKenzie, Heike Roms and C.J. Wee, in their introduction to *Contesting Performance* (2009), track the history of performance studies, mostly in the US. They discuss the binary opposition between theatre studies and performance studies, and challenge the, as they term it, "nested" structure of North American performance studies.[7] The centre of this structure contains Richard Schechner's "broad spectrum" performance studies, referring to connections made by Schechner and Victor Turner between anthropology and theatre, generally seen as a starting point for performance studies. For McKenzie et al., Schechner is nested in New York University's Performance Studies department, which is in turn nested in a specifically North American performance studies. The vigorous debate in American academia at the time of the emergence in the 1960's and subsequent institutionalisation in the 1980's of performance studies resulted eventually in a separation between theatre studies and performance studies. NYU and Northwestern University established the first Performance Studies departments, in 1980 and 1984 respectively. Throughout the second half of the twentieth-century, American institutions increasingly offered undergraduate degrees in either performance studies or theatre studies, and academics aligned themselves with one or the other. For example, Harrop vividly evokes the divisions apparent between performance studies and theatre/drama/dance/music studies at NYU and Brown, noted during a visit in 2003.[8] Indeed, as Shannon Jackson mentions in *Professing Performance: Theatre in the Academy from Philology to Performativity*, this partitioning came to a head in 1992, when Richard Schechner, in his keynote address at a conference run by the Association of Theatre in Higher Education, "called for the abolition of theatre departments" altogether.[9]

---

[8] Harrop, 196.
[9] Shannon Jackson, Professing Performance: Theatre in the Academy from Philology to Performativity (Cambridge: Cambridge University Press, 2004), 8.

Contrary to Schechner's assertion here, it seems that performance studies and theatre studies in the early part of this century continue to move around and through the various dichotomies to which they supposedly adhere, without the abolition of one or the other. As this chapter aims to articulate, an interesting example of the (re-) integration of the two fields can be placed alongside the introduction of the shift format to PSi conferences from 2009 onwards. In its stimulation of performative expressions of research—in a manner commensurate with the ongoing popularity of practice-based research and practice-as-research in both theatre studies and performance studies—the shift format stands as an additional bridge between the two fields, creating further points of access between the institutions, theoreticians, academics and practitioners that profess to subscribe to one or the other.

The auto-ethnographic writing in this chapter observes in an impressionistic way the correspondence between the opening up of the shift format, and a wider trend that continues to see performance studies and theatre studies in a state of co-existence rather than the opposing sides suggested by comments such as Schechner's above. For example, in 2003, Bottoms refers to the two fields as "dance partners" towards the end of his article, with the ability to support and understand each other, though with the caveat that "the dance is between mutually respectful equals."[10] This image remains an interesting approach to the relationship between the two fields, and the performative aspect corresponds to the discussion of the shift format throughout this chapter. It seems that an experiential noticing of the increased embedding of shifts into PSi conferencing contributes to a consideration of a similar movement by theatre studies and performance studies to extend beyond perceived dichotomies and divisions.

Shifts

As mentioned in the introduction, one of the purposes of this chapter is to note my experience of PSi shifts in 2009, 2011 and 2012 alongside the progression of the shift format's integration into the PSi conferences over the same period. While I did not attend the 2010 Toronto conference, and the 2013 Stanford conference is a number of months away at the time of writing, it seems that the written material surrounding these conferences may nevertheless be consulted despite the lack of experiential support that has been noted in evocations of the Zagreb, Utrecht and Leeds

---

[10] Bottoms, 185.

conferences. With this in mind, I will discuss fragments of the calls for papers and conference programmes of each conference, returning below to a more auto-ethnographic exploration of the shifts I have attended.

It is worth noting that, although the mention of the word "shift" in this context can be traced to the call for papers for the Zagreb conference in 2009, the roots of the idea can perhaps be seen a year earlier. Looking at the call for papers for PSi's 14th conference, "Interregnum: In Between States," in Copenhagen in 2008, I find no specific mention of what would become the shift format, though there is a sense that performative explorations of the conference themes are encouraged to an extent.[11] For example, I note that the call for papers "seeks papers, panels, and performances," though it gives no further information about how to submit a performance-based abstract, giving only details of the paper and panel proposal submission options.[12] Further to this, a scanned copy of the Copenhagen conference programme, available on the PSi website, reveals that "[a] number of panel sessions include both performances and academic presentations."[13] Additionally, a range of performance events appears to have taken place in tandem with the conference, though these are separated from the paper-based conference programme in the schedule.

However, turning to the PSi 15 (Zagreb) conference in 2009, an entire section of the conference website is labelled "PSi 15 Shifts." This section lays out the notion of the shift as a "non-conventional investigation of the conference themes," aiming to "accomplish a higher level of interaction between the participants in the conference and especially between artistic and theoretical work."[14] The writers of this section go on to acknowledge the fact that the integration of performative presentations into performance studies conferencing has long been attempted, but has struggled with

---

[11] It is also interesting to note that the last PSi conference before the shift format was introduced took the idea of interregnum as its principal theme. Speculatively, this theme presents an "in-between," not only as a rich subject, for discussion and debate, but also in terms of a future glance at the 2009 conference and the formal innovations that would be explored in Zagreb.
[12] Jiscmail, "PSi Archives," Jiscmail, https://www.jiscmail.ac.uk/cgi-bin/web admin?A2=PSI%3Bb1b3b7d2.0710 (accessed February 11, 2013).
[13] PSi website, "PSi 14 Programme," Performance Studies international, http://www.blogbird.nl/uploads/psi/130812084833923_psi14-program.pdf (accessed February 11, 2013) .
[14] Performance Studies international Conference, "PSi 15 Shifts," Performance Studies international, http://www.teatar.hr/psi15.com/?content=19 (accessed January 31, 2013).

"conventional conference spaces and schedules."[15] They further suggest that the shift format proposed for the Zagreb conference, and its recommendation that shift participants take performance (as distinct from the discursive mode of presentation) as their "organising principle," will endeavour to address these previous struggles. Suggestions for shift structures given by the Zagreb conference organisers include "performative presentations, round-table discussions on performances presented, workshops, interactive events, seminars, and even mini-symposia."[16] Further to this, they indicate that the shifts will take place during late afternoon, evening, or night-time.

This conference in Zagreb was entitled "MISPERFORMANCE: Misfiring, Misfitting, Misreading." Looking back over the enormous and unwieldy conference pack, I notice with interest in the context of this volume that a folklore researcher, Maja Bošković-Stulli, is credited with first introducing and translating into Croatian the term performance, having participated at a Helsinki conference on folk narrative research in 1974, where she first came in touch with American folklorists Dan Ben Amos and Alan Dundes, and their approaches to such work.[17] I am also drawn to a further explanation of the shifts, as here the conference organisers noted that their aim was to work towards a way of making "various forms of performance an equal and integral part of the conference programme."[18] While the choice of the word "shift" is not fully explained, the organisers (Morana Čale, Lada Čale Feldman, and Marin Blažević) make it clear in their discussion in the conference programme of "pivotal challenges of the PSi #15"[19] that they unequivocally intend the word to refer to a change, a shift, in the construction of a conference. They wonder about how to incorporate performance into the kinds of communication channels that any conference (hopefully) opens up. They think through how to improve the interaction and reflection between performance practices and the theories and criticism that such performance helps to strengthen and develop. So, in their own words, they settle on a format that "cannot be exclusively reduced to panels or working group meetings, roundtable discussions or workshops or lectures, work in progress presentations, public forums, interactive events, actions or installations,

---

[15] Ibid.
[16] Ibid.
[17] PSi 15, "Conference programme," (Performance Studies international conference, Zagreb, Croatia, 2009), 8.
[18] Ibid., 9.
[19] Ibid.

theatre or dance or performance art, multimedia performances, exhibitions, seminars or interventions."[20] Rather, the conference organisers seem to have concluded that shifts are combinations of those formats and genres, and experiments at their intersections, existing in between conventional or recognisable modes of "doing a conference," doing art, being a scholar,[21] being a practitioner.

And nowhere was an articulation of these intersections more recognisable than in a shift called "The School of Sisyphus." Curated by Rachel Fensham, Joe Kelleher, Ian Maxwell, and Monica Stufft, this shift, this school, took over an entire theatre building in the city centre. The list of participants, according to the conference pack, was a combination of theatre and performance studies academics, and live artists, and the shift description read as follows:

> This pedagogic shift has a utopian bent. It is concerned with the university to be, where participants construct a curriculum of crucial and peculiar studies. The focus of the School is not so much on a pre-established or vetted content but on people producing and engaging in opportunities for learning. We have invited individuals to profess performance in various ways (and with various pedagogical strategies).[22]

I arrive at the Zagreb Youth Theatre with others, and we are asked to sign up for the classes we wish to participate in throughout the evening, via a series of sign-up sheets adhered to a wall. Doors are labelled with the name of the tutor, and sometimes with the subject being taught inside. "Students" begin to drift from room to room, exploring familiar and unfamiliar ("crucial and peculiar") topics. For example, I enter Peter Eckersall's room, and the assembled group spends some time learning movements from the Japanese *kyogen* theatre. Laurie Beth Clark teaches me how to knit. I learn a Jewish wedding dance with Brian Lobel, and Richard Talbot provides an American-style high-school physical education class, complete with shouting, gum-chewing coach. Laura Cull gives me a partner and a page of Deleuze, and we read aloud to each other, slowly. Finally, Joe Kelleher and Rachel Fensham call the whole building to a madcap school assembly where work is demonstrated by students and reported on by teachers.

---

[20] Ibid.
[21] Ibid.
[22] Ibid., 47.

My attention is drawn to the theatricality of this participatory shift. Prepared characters, stuff happening behind the scenes, scripts, an interesting range of things that we associate with theatre. I am beginning to link this awareness of theatrical constructedness with the shift's descriptive statement, wondering perhaps whether the "utopian bent" to which the performer/organisers refer is as much a utopia of co-existence between theatre studies and performance studies as it is a utopia of pedagogic practice. I will return towards the end of this chapter to the opening panel of the Zagreb conference, and its surprisingly gentle acknowledgement of dissolving polarities between the two fields, but it seems that the conference's theme of misperformance is highlighting at a number of levels the many ways in which previously held dichotomies of theatre studies and performance studies have, in 2009, already been overcome. Noticeable, however, at this conference, is what might be thought of as a measured presence of the term "theatre," and the conventions, practices and theories associated with it. While not a complete absence, there is certainly a disinclination to discuss specifically theatre-based research at this particular conference, but this apparent reluctance is just one aspect of the relationship between the two fields that is to change very quickly over the three years following.

A year later, and PSi's 16th conference, entitled "Performing Publics" and held in Toronto in 2010, includes a separate paragraph for shift proposals in its call for papers. Building on the Zagreb definition of shifts above, the Toronto organisers describe the shifts as "innovative session formats that push the boundaries of the well-constructed panel."[23] Interestingly, this description includes a nod to theatre history's discussion of the well-made play, which suggests a tightly-constructed, often complex plot involving a dramatic build of suspense to a climax point, after which the problems of various characters are resolved into a happy ending.[24] This specific reference to theatre arguably builds on the points raised above about the ongoing incorporation of theatre studies and performance studies over this time period, parallel to the integration of the shift format into PSi conferences. However, it is also notable that this call

---

[23] Performance and Philosophy, "PSi 16—Toronto," Performance and Philosophy, http://psi-ppwg.wikidot.com/psi-16-toronto (accessed January 31, 2013).
[24] While it would be straying from the central concern of this chapter to further examine the links suggested in this call for papers between the well-made play and the "well-constructed panel," it remains an intriguing comparison, particularly a suggestion that the culmination of many (any?) conference panels represent a return to normality or a "happy ending."

for papers announces that "there will be a limited number of spaces for
shifts at PSi 16,"[25] a constraint not mentioned in the Zagreb information,
beyond a comment that there will not be more than three concurrent shifts
happening at any one time. This demarcation of space and time for shifts,
with no similar discussion of limitation applied to panel proposals, begins
to suggest a panel/shift dichotomy to a certain extent, perhaps with
traditional/innovative and basic requirements/demanding requirements as
new binaries to think through, according to the language used in the call
for papers.

The call for papers for the 2011 conference in Utrecht, "Camillo 2.0:
Technology, Memory, Experience," is similar to the 2009 and 2010
material in a number of ways. Shifts are defined as "alternative
presentational models that push the boundaries of the conference
presentation" and "non-conventional investigations into the themes of the
conference and are designed to accomplish a higher level of interaction
between the conference participants and especially between artistic and
theoretical work."[26] However, the "Camillo 2.0" team also presents a
subtle adjustment in the rhetoric that surrounds the discussions of shifts in
the 2009 and 2010 calls for papers and conference programmes. In a
general description of the Utrecht conference on the PSi 17 website, it is
noted that "[o]ver 50 shifts (demonstrations, installations, (lecture)
performances, workshops and discussions)" will be appearing at the
conference, with no further explanation of the shift format.[27] Similarly, the
sections of the conference programme detailing the scheduling of shifts are
simply titled "Shifts," with no qualifying paragraph or glossary. These
presentations occur in a range of venues scattered around Utrecht, thought
usually adjacent to the panel venues, and are visible in the programme
from 9am until 10pm. There is no announcement of spatial or temporal
limits to the shift format, as suggested in the Toronto written material. It
can be seen from this that as the shifts become increasingly assimilated
into the conference structure, the need to explain their presence becomes
unnecessary.

An interesting example of the ongoing disintegration of polarities
between theatre studies and performance studies is suggested in Utrecht. A

[25] "PSi 16—Toronto."
[26] Performance Studies international # 17, "Welcome to Camillo 2.0," Performance
Studies international # 17, http://www.psi17.org/page/home (accessed January 31,
2013).
[27] "Welcome to Camillo 2.0."

group of, to quote Richard Gough's description, "senior colleagues in our field, the elders and the elderly' propose a shift entitled 'Over the Hill: a rest home for performance studies scholars.'"[28] A small room was filled with performance studies books, televisions playing excerpts from performances, and visitors were invited to enter. The rest home's residents, who included Gough, Richard Schechner, Alan Read, Freddie Rokem, and others, offered some conversation stimuli, inviting a reminder "of what was once said; and what was once done but perhaps twice forgotten and many times misunderstood. To remind us of what still could be, and how it might appear differently."[29] For me, these are (or could be) considerations of the discipline, not only in the musings of its originators and progenitors, but in terms of its continuing relationship with theatre studies. Indeed, the notion of "performance studies scholars" retiring strikes me as particularly interesting in the light of this chapter's central discussion. While Gough, in his selection of participants, was clearly aligning "retirement" with age (and international profile), it seems worth noting that this could also refer to the retirement of a way of considering oneself a performance studies *or* theatre studies scholar, echoing the prelude panel at the Zagreb conference. This remains a tenuous connection between a shift primarily concerned with the forgetting and remembering done by scholars, and my impression of its notional relevance to the field(s) more generally. However, the prominent position occupied by shifts a year later at the Leeds conference further strengthens this idea, suggesting that this format continues to be indicative of wider reflections in both performance studies and theatre studies.

At the 2012 PSi conference in Leeds, shifts were integrated into the conference schedule at a deep structural level. Crucially, the call for proposals for this conference makes no differentiation between submissions of abstracts for paper panels or roundtable discussions, and submissions for more performative explorations of the conference theme. The conference organisers extend an invitation for "academics, artists and other practitioners to debate, develop, contest and celebrate the relationships between culture, industry and performance—now, in the past, and in possible futures."[30] Unlike the Utrecht announcement of a

---

[28] PSi 17, "Conference programme," (Performance Studies international conference, Utrecht, 2011), 27.
[29] Ibid.
[30] PSI # 18: performance, culture, industry, "Call for Proposals," PSI # 18: performance, culture, industry, http://www.pvac.leeds.ac.uk/psi18/call-for-proposals/ (accessed January 31, 2013).

specific number of shifts, or Toronto's assertion that only a certain number could be accommodated, the Leeds conference material makes no such statement. Furthermore, the conference theme certainly lends itself to an exploration of other meanings of the word "shift," relating to a shift of work perhaps, though when I return to the conference programme, I can find no explicit articulations of this. Indeed, it is only in "Night Shift Drifts," a shift co-curated by Simon Bayly, Charlie Fox, and Cecilia Wee in Zagreb in 2009, that I can find a definite use of the word in a context outside of the conference's definition.[31]

Shifts at this 18th PSi conference are scheduled throughout the conference day and in a range of spaces throughout the university campus. The conference programme organises by theme, with each contribution corresponding to Articulations, Commercial, Ecology, Relations, Training or Value.[32] In terms of form, a scheduled event is either Shift, Paper Panel, Curated Panel, Roundtable or Meeting. Thus, the opening of any page of the conference programme at random reveals approximately 25 events, with an average of 8-10 shifts. The notion that about one third of the PSi conference would be programmed for shift presentations by 2012 shows a swift build from the original 2009 suggestions made by the Zagreb organisers, a growing demand to be able to articulate research in a range of ways that do not necessarily conform to discursive practices or settings.

Taking this examination of the conference material further, it was also interesting to note that a number of sessions, positioned as shifts in the Leeds programme, approached the curated panel or roundtable format in their internal structure, with individual (extended) papers followed by a discussion. This seems to suggest the notion that the submission of a proposal (approximately 8 months in advance of the conference) to create a shift, rather than a paper panel or curated panel, perhaps allowed participants a potential freedom from the perceived constraints of the panel format, suggested in the rhetoric used by the Zagreb, Toronto and Utrecht organisers, without necessarily having to completely utilise those freedoms in the eventual construction of the event for the conference. A further point of interest relates to the wealth of paper panels, shifts, and roundtable discussions involving theatre and theatre studies at the PSi Leeds conference. Drawing comparisons between the 2009 and 2012 programmes, there are no references to theatre in the titles of any of the

---

[31] PSi 15, "Conference programme," 62.
[32] PSi 18, "Conference programme," (Performance Studies international conference, 2012), 2.

Zagreb conference contributions, and nine shifts / panels / roundtables specifically focused on theatre at the Leeds conference. Additionally, the conference organisers in Leeds programmed a performing arts festival in conjunction with the conference, and the performances on offer ranged from theatrical interpretations of dramatic text to live art to dance.

At the time of writing, the only information I have about the shift format at PSi's 19th conference, which will take place at Stanford University in June 2013, is to be found in the call for papers. Here, in their announcement of "praxis sessions" and "performance proposals," the organisers articulate an alignment with previous years, particularly the Zagreb and Utrecht frameworks, for the integration of shifts into the conference, and also discuss some points of contrast. To begin with, the language used to describe the praxis sessions recalls aspects of the language used in the descriptions of shifts above. For the Stanford organising team, "[t]he format of praxis sessions is designed to promote and facilitate rigorous reflection on performance presented by means other than traditional conference panels."[33] Additionally, in their assimilation of the roundtable discussion format into the paper panels side of the conference, the organisers can note that "it is just as important to know what a praxis session is as what it is *not*. A praxis session is *not* an expanded panel, a roundtable, or a stand-alone performance."[34] This directional language provides an interesting point of contrast with that used in the Leeds conference material, where differentiation between shifts, curated panels and roundtables was only noted (for the conference attendee) at the point of scheduling. However, the outcome of the language used in this call for papers remains to be seen, and the mapping of the praxis sessions in Stanford onto the trajectory of the shift format at PSi conferences from 2009-2012 could perhaps represent a further opportunity to ethnographise.

In Leeds in 2012, I return now, briefly, to the first shift I described above. Broderick Chow, who has been training in WWE wrestling for the past year, has developed this shift piece, entitled "Work Songs,"[35] alongside Tom Wells and Louise Owen. A physical comedy/dance piece exploring an office workplace, it examines physical labour in an exciting

---

[33] Performance Studies international conference 19, "Praxis Sessions," Performance Studies international conference 19, https://psi19.stanford.edu/cfp/praxis (accessed January 31, 2013).
[34] "Praxis Sessions."
[35] PSi 18, "Conference programme," 15.

way. The long period of wrestling between the two male performers leaves them both breathless and sweating profusely. It reminds me of the work of another kind that has stretched the confines of the PSi conference to this point. Back in Zagreb in 2009, somewhat breathless from the long days of thought and talk (traditional style paper panels during the day gave way in that first experimental year to shifts from late afternoon to half past midnight), those who remained for the Annual General Meeting on the last day in Zagreb agreed that the shift format would remain a feature of PSi conferences, as has been shown above. The work continues to be worthwhile.

Conclusions

In conclusion, this chapter has attempted to relate the establishment of the shift format at PSi conferences since 2009 to an ongoing (re-)blurring of a range of performance studies/theatre studies dichotomies. Using material from conference packs and calls for papers, and interspersing it with an impressionistic, auto-ethnographic writing that focuses on a personal experience of shifts at some of these conferences, I have aimed to suggest a way of mapping this aspect of PSi over the past number of years onto my own considerations of the fields. Indeed, examining aspects of this chapter's methodology, it is perhaps possible to suggest that the auto-ethnographic approach to the shifts described above, pieces that in many ways were concerned with theatricality and mimesis, further emphasises the fading of lines previously drawn between performance studies' anthropological roots, and theatre studies' textual and aesthetic origins. Returning, once more, to Zagreb in 2009, and to the conference's opening panel, "Zagreb Friendly Fire: Theatre Studies and Performance Studies," I note panel member Patrice Pavis' handout to the assembled audience, entitled "Dichotomies we must overcome (for an armistice)." A number of items on Pavis' list were discussed by six prominent theatre studies and performance studies scholars during this panel, including theatre studies' supposed privileging of text versus performance studies' supposed primary concern with the body; the respective fields' articulations of the relationship between theory and practice; and differing perspectives on perceived institutional or educational norms and how each field subverts, challenges, complies with or perpetuates them. The panellists (Janelle Reinelt, Hans-Thies Lehmann, Patrice Pavis, Richard Gough, Jill Dolan, Joe Roach) reached across the subjects of professionalisation of graduate students, questions of genealogy, the combining of the personal and the political, the laboratory aspect of theatre and performance, acknowledging the re-treading of ground and the re-asking of questions that are at least as old as performance studies itself.[36] The continued celebration of each discipline, the suggestion of "theatre-performance" as an all-encompassing field, and the agreed impotence of many of the binaries suggested on Pavis' list, indicated what the introduction and rise of the shift format at PSi conferences appears to have confirmed. These perceived dichotomies continue to collapse, and the formal foundation of new ways of presenting research that encourage theatrical and/or performative expression accentuates this decline, invoking not just Pavis' "armistice" between fields, but an increasingly productive co-existence.

Works Cited

Bottoms, Stephen. "The Efficacy/Effeminacy Braid: Unpicking the Performance Studies/Theatre Studies Dichotomy." *Theatre Topics* 13, no. 2 (2003): 173-187.

EFestivals. "Ghostfest '12'" EFestivals, http://www.efestivals.co.uk/festivals/ghostfest/2012.

Harrop, Peter. "'What's in a name?'" *Studies in Theatre and Performance* 25, (2005): 189-200.

Jackson, Shannon. *Professing Performance: Theatre in the Academy from Philology to Performativity*. Cambridge: Cambridge University Press, 2004.

Jiscmail. "PSi Archives" Jiscmail. https://www.jiscmail.ac.uk/cgi-bin/web admin?A2=PSI%3Bb1b3b7d2.0710.

McKenzie, Jon., Heike Roms., and C.J. W-L Wee. eds. *Contesting Performance: Global Sites of Research*. Basingstoke: Palgrave Macmillan, 2009.

Performance and Philosophy. "PSi 16 – Toronto." Performance Studies international, http://psi-ppwg.wikidot.com/psi-16-toronto.

Performance Studies international conference #14. "PSi 14 Programme." Performance Studies international, http://www.psi-web.org/detail/posts/11105.

Performance Studies international conference #15. "PSi 15 Shifts." Performance Studies international, Zagreb, Croatia, June 2009.

Performance Studies international conference #15, http://www.teatar.hr/psi15.com/?content=19.

Performance Studies international conference #17. Conference programme. Performance Studies international, Utrecht, Holland, May, 2011.

---

[36] PSi 15, "Conference programme," 15.

Performance Studies international #17. "Welcome to Camillo 2.0."
    Performance Studies international #17,
    http://www.psi17.org/page/home.
Performance Studies international conference 19. "Praxis Sessions."
    Performance Studies international Conference 19,
    https://psi19.stanford.edu/cfp/praxis.
PSi #15: (Mis) Performance Studies international conference 15.
    Conference programme. Performance Studies international, Zagreb,
    Croatia, June, 2009.
PSi #18: performance, culture, industry. "Call for Proposals." PSi #18:
    performance, culture, industry, http://www.pvac.leeds.ac.uk/psi18/call-
    for-proposals/.
PSi #18: performance, culture, industry. Conference programme.
    Performance Studies international, Leeds, UK, June, 2012.
Read, Alan. "Programme note for *The White Estuary*." Handout
    distributed by the author, Performance Studies international, Leeds,
    UK, June, 2012.
Research Excellent Framework. Accessed 31 January 2013.
    http://www.ref.ac.uk/.

CONTRIBUTORS

Jane Bacon is Professor of Dance, Performance and Somatics at University of Chichester, UK. She is Co-Director of The Choreographic Lab and Joint Editor of *Choreographic Practices Journal*. Her research in 'self as creative source' for practice-led research in performance has taken her on a journey from improvised dance and screen work to auto-ethnography and on to a mindful practice of body, mind and spirit. She is also a Jungian analyst in training, an Authentic Movement practitioner and Focusing Trainer.

Ann R David is Head of Department of Dance at the University of Roehampton where she specialises in Dance Anthropology, South Asian studies, and popular dance forms. She gained her Ph.D in Dance Ethnography at De Montfort University after completing an MA (Dist) in Dance Studies at the University of Surrey. She has been a Research Fellow on the international research project, *'The Religious Lives of Ethnic and Immigrant Minorities: A Transnational Perspective'*, based in London, Kuala Lumpur and Johannesburg, funded by the Ford Foundation, USA.

Peter Harrop is Professor in Drama at the University of Chester and currently Pro-Vice Chancellor. He gained his degrees in Drama, Education and Folklore at the University of Leeds (Ph.D. 1980) and previously taught theatre arts at the University of Addis Ababa (1980 – 1985) and Bretton Hall (1985 – 1996). He has published in *Lore and Language*; *Folk Life: A Journal of Ethnological Studies*; *Studies in Theatre and Performance*; *Performance Research*; *Popular Entertainment Studies* and *Contemporary Theatre Review*.

Dunja Njaradi is postdoctoral research fellow in the Department of Performing Arts, University of Chester. She holds degrees from Belgrade (BA Ethnology), Nottingham (MA Slavonic Studies) and Lancaster (PhD Theatre Studies) and is associate editor of *Journal of Dance, Movement and Spiritualties*. As a theatre and dance studies scholar she works within several interdisciplinary affiliations: physical theatre, dance anthropology and contemporary dance.

Ben Power is an ethnomusicologist and Irish traditional musician and dancer from New Brighton on Merseyside. Currently in the Integrative Studies in Music program at the University of California, San Diego, he took M.A.s at the University of Limerick (Plainchant and Irish Traditional Music performance). He has produced two recordings of Irish traditional music, *The Mouse in the Mug* and *Traditional Irish Music on Flute and Fiddle*, and teaches Irish traditional music performance and pedagogy privately, in the academy, and at festivals internationally.

Karen Quigley is Lecturer in Drama and Theatre Studies at the University of Chester. She is currently completing her doctorate at King's College London under the supervision of Professor Alan Read, exploring ideas of unstageability and limitation in 20th century theatre. Karen has published work in *Performance Research* and *Platform*, and is an Associate of Trinity College London (Piano Performance).

Paul Smith is a Professor of Folklore at Memorial University in Newfoundland. He instigated the Traditional Drama Conferences series at the University of Sheffield in 1978 and co-edited *Traditional Drama Studies* (1985-1996). His most recent works in this area are with Eddie Cass, *The Peace Egg Chapbook in Lancashire* (in press), and with Michael J. Preston, *Sir Walter Scott and the Sword Dance From Papa Stour in Shetland, Including a Facsimile of James Scott's 1829 Manuscript, "The Sword Dance: A Danish or Norwegian Ballet, &c, As Performed in the Island of Papa Stour, Zetland"* (forthcoming).

INDEX